BLANK PAGE
TO BOOKSHELF

From First Sentence to First Sale: Fiction Writing,
Character Creation, and Self-Publishing Basics

MARK McNEASE

Copyright © 2026 Mark McNease
Published by MadeMark Publishing
Stockton, New Jersey
Cover design by MadeMark Publishing
ISBN: 979-8-9942675-0-9

This book is intended as a guide to writing and self-publishing. The author and publisher make no representations or warranties with respect to the accuracy or completeness of the contents of this work and disclaim all warranties. The advice and strategies contained herein may not be suitable for your situation.

Table of Contents

Part I: Fiction Essentials
Chapter 1: Why Didn't I Think of That?
Chapter 2: I Have an Idea, Now What?
Chapter 3: Genres (So You Want To Write a –)
Chapter 4: Inside the Outline
Chapter 5: A Matter of Perspective (POV)
Chapter 6: Creating Suspense
Chapter 7: Dialogue
Chapter 8: Exposition
Chapter 9: Getting Input, Mentors, and Peers

Part II: They're Alive! Creating Vivid Characters
Chapter 10: Understanding Key Elements of Character
Chapter 11: The Character Biography
Chapter 12: New Worlds Yet to Be Imagined

Part III: Doing It All: Self-Publishing
Chapter 13: Brave Not-So-New World
Chapter 14: You're Ready to Publish, Now What?
Chapter 15: What It Looks Like
Chapter 16: Under the Covers: Making a First Impression
Chapter 17: More On Covers: DIY or Outsource?
Chapter 18: Formatting the Paperback Edition
Chapter 19: Go Tell It On The Mountain
Chapter 20: Hearing is Believing: A Word on Audiobooks
Chapter 21: Thick Skin and a Lot of Determination
About Mark McNease

What They're Saying

"I've been working with Mark on my autobiography for several months. He is insightful, talented, and a wonderful asset in bringing my life's story to the page. He made it possible and pleasant. And fun!" – K.C.

"5 Stars for an informative, and inspiring online workshop given by Mark McNease. The well organized 2 hour workshop provided just the right amount of content to help writers begin their creative path. As an author of three books I found this course provided new insights into the craft of writing as well as reinforced others that needed a refresh." – Robert M.

"Level up your writing game! I recently took this workshop and transformed my skills. McNease is a pro – always as an author I've long enjoyed, and now as an instructor. His knowledge and passion for writing are infectious." – Rick R.

"I'm just beginning to dabble in fiction writing, so I was nervous about participating in Mark's workshop, worried that I would not belong among more-experienced writers. It turns out that I had nothing to worry about! I was warmly welcomed and encouraged by Mark and the other participants. Mark's workshop was logically organized, well-paced, and packed with useful information. I highly, highly (yes, that's repetitive) recommend this workshop for anybody interested in beginning or moving forward in their writing journey. You won't be disappointed." – Amanda M.

"I had a blast! Mr. McNease's workshop was a revelation. His ability to quickly break through this writer's inhibition and get you to simply write is refreshing. He quickly set my mind at ease! Highly recommend him." – Al M.

"As someone who isn't a writer, I was a bit nervous about attending this workshop. I needn't have been, because the relaxed and convivial

tone Mark set had me feeling like I was at a retreat rather than a classroom. He employed thought-provoking prompts which stirred something within me, and I not only did some writing but I thoroughly enjoyed the process. I'd happily recommend his workshops to anyone looking for an out-of-the-box way to connect with themselves or others."
– Randi S.

"Mark McNease's KDP workshop takes a potentially overwhelming path to self-publishing and makes it both practical and manageable. The workshop covers the most salient points for navigating the KDP site and addresses tips for avoiding glitches with fonts and formats. Mark provides materials to reinforce the presentation and tales of his own fifteen-year journey in the self-publishing world. I highly recommend the experience for both beginning and seasoned writers." - Victoria Short, author of Find Your Mini Pumpkin

Also by the Author

Writing as M.A. McNease

I, Warlock: The Warlock Wars Book I
A House in the Woods
A House in the Woods 2
Hell to Pay

Writing as Mark McNease

Mysteries and Thrillers
Night Flight to Murder Town
Open Secrets: A Maggie
Reservation for Murder
Beautiful Corpse
Black Cat White Paws
Murder at Pride Lodge
Pride and Perilous
Death in the Headlights
Death by Pride
Kill Switch
Last Room at the Cliff's Edge

Audiobooks
Night Flight to Murder Town
Open Secrets
Reservation for Murder
Beautiful Corpse
A House in the Woods
Black Cat White Paws
Murder at Pride Lodge
Pride and Perilous
Death by Pride
Death in the Headlights
Last Room at the Cliff's Edge

Stop the Car

Other Books and Writing
Tunda: Short Fiction from 2000 - -2022
Stop the Car: A Kindle Single
The Seer: A Short Story
Rough & Tumble: A Dystopian Love Tragedy
An Unobstructed View: Short Fiction
5 of a Kind: More Short Fiction

Dedication

For my mentors
Bob Delegall and Sal Romeo
somewhere across the universe.

And for all the others who teach us
to believe in ourselves.

Introduction

Once upon a time there was a boy with a vivid imagination—some might say wild—who loved the astonishing variety of worlds offered to him in books and stories. He was very fond of reading Edgar Allan Poe and Nathanial Hawthorn, highlighting all the big words they used, which he would then look up in a dictionary. It expanded both his ability to envision all these worlds, and his own vocabulary. He was determined not to be left behind just because he didn't know the meanings of 'tertiary' or 'circumlocution,' or 'succinct.' It was like learning a foreign language he already spoke, a set of keys to mysterious passageways leading away from his everyday life into places that had been unimaginable the day before.

The boy knew by the age of ten that he, too, wanted to create worlds that first existed in his mind. He wanted to detail them, populate them, and color them in with words. He started writing short stories in spiral notebooks, and by the time he was a teenager his fate was sealed. He would write or cease to exist. Creating was both his only way in, and his only way *out*. Out of the challenges a young boy faces. Out of the confusion, out of the grey areas. He knew what salvation was—he'd been to church many times—and he knew the written word would be his.

Many years later, he offers what he's learned in this slim volume: the essentials of fiction writing, how to create characters who are as alive as the man driven mad by the beating of a heart beneath the floorboards, or a woman brought up among a family of circus freaks, or a widow solving murders in a small river town. How to take what's been written and publish it, from ebook to paperback to audiobook. And how to get from 'Blank Page to Bookshelf' with determination, discipline, and a very wild imagination.

- Mark McNease

Actually, You Can

I have several talismans situated around my writing desk: a Day of the Dead skull I got in Mexico City on a business trip long ago; an Edgar Allan Poe pendant dangling on a nail; a wooden heart with wings spreading out to the sides. The two Emmys for co-creating and writing a children's program (*Into the Outdoors*) don't really count as talismans, but they don't hurt. They raise their globes to the ceiling on shelves just above my sight line.

Another creative helper, if you will, is a small wooden block with the words 'Actually, I Can' written on it. I loved it the instant I saw it, and I fastened it to the corkboard on the wall above my computer monitor. Long before I bought it in a local shop, I'd believed it to be true. *Actually, I can.* I've believed it since I was a teenager who was certain I wanted to be a writer. I've never been an imposter and don't indulge in thinking I am. Perhaps beginning to write at the age of ten, and knowing it was both my rescue and the one thing I would want to do my entire life, the through line of it all, helped me be sure. There have been many times I've wondered if I could finish something I was writing, but never a moment's doubt that I could write.

This book is the product of fifty years of writing, and fifteen years of self-publishing. Being both highly controlling and someone who always worked 'a regular job' until two years ago, I had to learn to do it all—graphic arts for cover design, publishing platforms from Kindle Direct Publishing (KDP), to IngramSpark, to ACX for audiobooks, to website design, to promotion and advertising. I refer to myself as a one-person production company, and that's very true. It's also very rewarding.

To the voice in my head that occasionally told me I just couldn't do this, I say, *Actually, I can.*

And so can you.

Why We Write

If you're reading this, there's a better than even chance you're a writer, or you want to be one, or you're somewhere along the transition between dreaming it and making it so. My personal conviction is that *a writer writes*, just as a dancer dances and a painter paints. Who tells someone painting on a canvas or drawing on paper that they cannot claim to be a painter or artist until they've had their own gallery show? Or even until they sell a painting? Who tells someone twirling on a dancefloor that they cannot be a dancer until they've debuted on a stage or been paid for their movements through space and time? *If you write, you are a writer.* You may be somewhere on a scale from aspiring to accomplished (however you define that), but when you put words to paper you are a writer. Accept it. Embrace it. Don't doubt it. It's one thing to question the quality of what you've written, but never question that you've written it.

I know there is disagreement about this. I know there are a great many people, especially in the publishing industry, that maintain you are not a writer, and certainly not an author, until you have an agent, or a book deal with a traditional publisher, or some other official recognition and validation, and they're free to think that. But remember you are also free to ignore it. The sooner we acknowledge our own writer-ness, the sooner we can let go of confining ourselves and our sense of accomplishment to what other people expect.

In my workshops, I emphasize that I consider it my job, and my duty, to encourage participants to explore their creativity with writing. That's why they're taking the workshop. Some of them have never written before, while others have novels in drawers, and still others have published their stories and books. Expressing ourselves with writing can be a fragile and precious thing. I would never want to discourage anyone. Who am I to do that, anyway? I want to be a nurturer, a bit of nutrient and water and sunshine, allowing the participants' imagination and confidence to grow.

Sometimes what comes from this fertile soil is a finished work ready to be published. That's what this book is about: how to take that world you've created and make it available for everyone to visit.

Fiction Essentials

There's a reason those of us who write fiction choose this form of literary expression as opposed to, say, biography, or history, or essays. To write fiction is to design worlds that did not exist before we brought them forth from the depths of our creativity. That's certainly why I started on this path. I was a child who loved to read, learn new words, and delight in all the new adventures I went on between the pages of books. There was something very transporting about reading an Edgar Allan Poe story, or heading off into the galaxy with Frank Herbert. I could dare myself to enter the horror of a Stephen King story, or its scientific twin by Michael Crighton (*Andromeda Strain* was quite a thrill to this 11-year-old when it was first published). My equal love of literary fiction came later with James Baldwin, Katherine Dunn, Toni Morrison, Alice Walker and so many more. In my teens I devoured poetry by contemporary masters of the form, from Charles Bukowski to Nikki Giovanni. (I always tell writers if they want to develop a better ear, read poetry. It teaches us economy of language, as well as pacing, rhythm and sound.)

Writing, like reading, can offer us a way of understanding an often incomprehensible world. *Especially for children.* My love of books made trips to the library among my favorite outings. Later it became browsing a bookstore—any bookstore—and that remains the case all these years later. Few things enthrall me like entering a room filled with books and seeing all those colorful spines, each one an invitation to go *somewhere.*

To write fiction is to be the person offering that invitation to ourselves and to others. It says, *Follow me, I'm about to head off to a most marvelous place, with interesting people who have amazing stories to tell. Let's go!* We're the ticket taker and the guide, and we are always the first in line.

Something to Try

As we approach the entrance, the first step of this journey into the how and why, let's stop to consider why we're going on it.

- Write about *why you write*. What motivated you to want to do this? Was it something you've desired since childhood, or did it offer itself to you later in life?
- What do you think writing *is*?
- What kind of writing do you currently do, or want to do? And *why*?
- What do you want to get out of it? Is it a solitary pleasure, or something you want to offer the world?

Are you prepared to do the work? If you're already doing it, know there is always more

Why Didn't I Think Of That?

Every story starts with an idea. Where do these ideas come from? You may overhear a conversation in a diner and begin spinning it into a tale in your story-mind. Or you may see a poster on a utility pole searching for a missing cat. *Black Cat White Paws*, with a photograph of the cat and a phone number to reach its panicked owner. Or an empty swimming pool where suddenly you envision a dead body at the bottom. It was fall, and the pool had been emptied. All it held was a pile of brown leaves and a dead man near the drain. How did he get there? Was he murdered?

The desire to write is the desire to tell a story: whether it's fictional, or even if it's your own story in the form of a memoir or autobiography. Fiction is often a little bit of both. The dictum to 'write what you know' can simply mean writing about your own environment, locating your stories in the city or town you live in. It can also mean creating characters that have at least a passing resemblance to people you're familiar with, either intimately or by acquaintance. How much you choose to fictionalize these characters and these places is up to you. When I wrote a horror story I changed the name of the local town it was based on, simply because the story had a lot of bad people in it and I consider my neighbors to be good for the most part. If they have relationships with the Devil, they've never revealed that to me.

The people and places we know also have a way of showing up in our writing without us intending them to. A place name comes to mind, or a character trait gets displayed that seems oddly familiar to us. It's okay. Unless we're basing locations and characters on real people, there's no need to worry they'll find out. They may even be flattered.

I like to write what I know in terms of the towns and cities I've lived in: Elkhart, Indiana, or Los Angeles, or New York, and now near Lambertville, New Jersey, and the surrounding areas. I often say my characters all strangely moved here after I did. It works for me. It may not work for you, and that's for you to discover and determine as you set about telling your own tall or not-so-tall tales.

A question you may hear often is, 'Is this autobiographical?' Hopefully it won't be asked about a serial killer or vampire, but you may encounter it a lot – especially if you're writing an autobiography. People have a natural curiosity about what we do as writers. Some of them think it's magical, while others think pretty much anyone can do it. While I've said I believe a writer writes, there is a great deal of skill, learning and practice that are required for progressing in your craft, or developing the kind of discipline and practice that can result in people wanting to read what you wrote. While it's true that anyone can publish these days, it's not true that anyone can gain an audience with what they've published.

My goal with this book is to guide the reader through the process of creating fiction that's rewarding to write, attractive to readers, and that has the potential to at least supplement an income, if not be its main source. And it all starts with an idea—a seed that you either planted yourself or had planted by a chance experience or even an obsession.

Something to Try

- Where do *your* ideas comes from?
- Write out, in a few sentences or paragraphs, ideas you have or have had for a story.
- Who is the protagonist/central character?
- What/where is the environment?
- Why does this story matter to you?

What is your beginning, middle, and end?

I Have An Idea, Now What?

Character is story, and story is character. There is a symbiosis between your characters and your story. They can't really be separated. It would be like recalling your experiences with the townspeople in a town where no one lived. A story without character is like a balloon without air, or an empty bowl set in front of a hungry person who is then given a spoon and told to enjoy it. Conversely, a character without a story is the soup without a bowl, the air without the balloon, and the townspeople without a town.

Note that character and plot are two different things, while at the same time informing each other. A well-developed character will find a way of wriggling outside your mind and making some decisions on their own. I've often been surprised when a character insisted on taking a right turn when I had fully intended them to go left. Sometimes they surprise you with actions, words and intentions you had not anticipated—and by taking over the story if they want it to go somewhere else. While you can't have one without the other, you build the house they will live in, and you decide what is behind each door. Character and story are two central limbs of the same tree that grows from your imagination. As we create one, we also create the other.

Developing a character—or characters—is a way of developing story. Either can come first.

Let's say you have a story idea. Let's say it's a poster on a utility pole looking for a lost cat. Let's say it strikes you for some reason, and the central mystery of it—where is the cat? Who is searching for it? How could it be explored in a murder mystery?—nags at you to the point you want to write a story about it. Then what?

Someone has to tell your story. In most cases that someone is the protagonist. The main character, or 'MC.' This is the person around whom the story will be constructed. Let's start with them.

Who Do You Need To Tell Your Story?

A protagonist – what do they want?
    Why must they tell this story?
    What is at stake?

An antagonist – the equal and opposing force.
    Who will try to stop your protagonist? A villain? A holder of secrets? A jealous lover? Someone who is at opposite purposes with your main character.

Your Protagonist

Some Classic and Modern Protagonists

1. Elizabeth Bennet, Jane Austen's sharp, self-aware heroine from *Pride and Prejudice*.
2. Sherlock Holmes – The iconic detective from Sir Arthur Conan Doyle.
3. Frodo Baggins – Tolkien's quiet, reluctant hero who proves that bravery isn't about strength alone.
4. Katniss Everdeen – A survival-driven heroine from Suzanne Collins's *The Hunger Games*.
5. Lisbeth Salander – A fiercely intelligent, unconventional heroine from Stieg Larsson's crime novels.

Who characters are usually dictates the choices they make, the actions they take, and the reactions of others. That all combusts in the flame of our imagination to create the story these characters are telling. It may sound cliché, but motivation is central to character and to story. If your character is running away from home, for instance, why is she doing that? And by making that choice, new possibilities will arise: what possesses or compels her to flee? Is she running *from* something, or *toward* something? Or both?

Does she take a bus, or a train? Does she drive, or walk? What are the differences? Would she meet the same people on a train as she would driving a car? If she's driving, whose car is it? And would she meet anyone at all? She's behind a wheel, in an enclosed vehicle. Perhaps she picks up a hitchhiker, or a friend in the middle of the night who is helping her or joining her.

Who she is, what she has experienced, and the story her actions are telling all combine to create a whole.

What They Want

What does your character want enough to propel them through the story? Even the autobiographer *wants* something: to set the record straight, to preserve their story for posterity, to pursue catharsis, to educate or entertain. A story without a reason is not a story people will want to read.

Why They Must Tell This Story

It's not just another day. Today—the days of the story—is unique and urgent, even if it's a quiet urgency. A good story has the feeling that it could not have been told at any other time. The dead body floated up today, and had it not, or had it been carried downstream, everything might be different.

As the unseen narrator, you and your characters share a need to tell this story *now*. It begins, proceeds, and ends within a unique timeframe. And that time frame demands that this story be told within it. The more a story feels as if it must be told now, and by these characters, the stronger it will be.

The Stakes And The Stakeholders

Characters who desire something bring energy and purpose to a story. Their wants serve as the driving force behind their decisions and actions, giving readers a reason to invest in their journey. Whether it's a quest for love, justice, freedom, or self-understanding, a character's yearning propels the plot forward and makes their experience relatable. Without a clear desire, a character risks feeling passive or static, draining the story of momentum and emotional engagement.

Desire also introduces conflict, which is essential to storytelling. When a character wants something, obstacles inevitably arise—be it opposition from other characters, internal struggles, or external circumstances. These barriers not only create tension and suspense, but also offer opportunities for growth and change. The process of pursuing and potentially achieving their goals allows characters to evolve, revealing new facets of their personalities and deepening their relationships with others.

A character's desires reflect the themes and messages of the story. Their pursuit highlights what matters most in the narrative world you've created and invites readers to question their own values and motivations. A well-defined objective transforms the character into more than just a plot device; it makes them a living, breathing individual whose story must be told.

Your Antagonist

Some Classic and Modern Antagonists

1. Iago, from Shakespear's Othello, a jealous ensign who engineers Othello's downfall.
2. Sauron, Tolkein's Dark Lord of Middle-earth, with his quest for absolute power.
3. Nurse Ratched, the mental institution's nurse from *One Flew Over the Cuckoo's Nest*.
4. Hannibal Lecter, among the most famous, from *The Silence of the Lambs*.
5. Annie Wilkes, from Stephen King's *Misery*, whose obsession with a novelist turns violent.

An antagonist is a character, force, or entity that stands in direct opposition to the protagonist. This opposition can manifest in various forms, including a classic villain, a rival, a natural disaster, societal norms, or even the protagonist's own internal struggles. The antagonist's role is not necessarily to be evil, but to create obstacles that challenge the protagonist's desires and goals. By doing so, the antagonist becomes a catalyst for conflict and a driving force within the narrative.

The presence of an antagonist is essential because it generates tension and stakes, which are critical elements of compelling storytelling. Without an opposing force, the protagonist's journey would lack urgency and depth, making the story feel flat or aimless. The antagonist forces the protagonist to make difficult choices, confront their weaknesses, and rise to new levels of determination and ingenuity. This friction between opposing forces is what keeps readers engaged, as they become invested in how the protagonist will overcome the challenges presented.

An effective antagonist can highlight the core themes and

messages of a story. By reflecting or contrasting the protagonist's values and motivations—good versus evil, hero versus villain—the antagonist adds complexity and suspense to the story. Their presence pushes the protagonist—and, by extension, the reader—to question what is truly right or necessary. Did your hero really have to take a particular action to achieve their goal? Did they behave unethically, or put an innocent person at risk? What are the ambiguities of your protagonist's choices and the consequences of them?

Antagonists are not just obstacles to be defeated; they are integral to the emotional and philosophical richness of a story, shaping its direction and impact from beginning to end.

Who will try to stop your protagonist? A villain? A holder of secrets? A jealous lover? What or who is the equal and opposing force?

Something to Try

List a few protagonists and their opposing antagonists. What is the protagonist determined to achieve, and why is the antagonist determined to thwart them?

- Identify some protagonist / antagonist parings from literature or film you can easily identify (Professor Moriarty versus Sherlock Holmes; the Witch versus Dorothy; the alien versus Ellen Ripley).
- What did they want in opposition to each other? (To defeat the adversary; to reclaim the slippers; the survive as an alien species).

How were they a equal and opposing forces?

Genre: So You Want To Write A [Romance, Mystery, Thriller]

There aren't many things we can just *do*, having never done them before. Writing is craft, and craft takes study as well as practice. Are you writing a murder mystery? What are the general rules of mysteries? What are the rules of mysteries' sub-genres (cozies, hardboiled, amateur sleuth, procedural)? What are the rules of the genre you want work in, including autobiography? Literary fiction, too, has rules, even if they're less formulaic.

Whatever story you decide to tell needs a clear beginning, middle, and end. This classic structure provides readers with a sense of orientation and progression, giving the narrative a logical flow. The beginning introduces the world, characters, and the initial situation or conflict, laying the groundwork for everything that follows. Without a strong opening, readers may feel lost or uninvested, struggling to understand the stakes or motivations that drive the story forward. As a reader as well as a writer, being drawn in after the first page or two is a sign that I'm about to go on an interesting journey. Likewise, if I'm not interested by the time I've read a few pages, it's likely I won't continue reading. This applies to writing as well: if I'm not interested in my own story, I can't expect anyone else to be.

The middle of a story is where the action unfolds and complications arise, challenging the protagonist and developing the central conflict. This section is crucial for building tension, deepening characterization, and exploring the themes introduced at the outset. The middle acts as a bridge between the introduction and the resolution, ensuring that events do not happen in isolation but are meaningfully connected. It is here that the protagonist faces obstacles, makes pivotal decisions, and experiences transformation, all of which keep readers engaged and eager to see what happens next.

Finally, the ending provides closure, resolving the conflicts and questions raised earlier in the narrative. Whether the conclusion is triumphant, tragic, or open-ended, it gives the story a sense of purpose and completion. A satisfying ending allows readers to reflect on the journey, understand the implications of the characters' choices, and appreciate the overarching message or theme. If you're writing a series, the ending is also where the reader is enticed to keep following your protagonist to the next book.

Without a definitive end, even the most well-crafted story can feel incomplete, leaving readers unsatisfied and disconnected from the narrative's impact.

Something to Try

Write out the beginning, middle, and end of your story. If you don't have one yet, start now. Describe each of these three elements with at least one paragraph, but feel free to include more. And remember the benefits of brevity: you can fill in the details later. For the moment, write out the story as if you are telling someone what it's about and you have just a few minutes to do it.

Know The Rules Before You Break Them

While every genre has at least a loose set of rules and expectations to follow, it doesn't mean you can't break them, provided you know them first. An example I often use is the romance genre. It's among the most popular, and most restrictive, of the various genres you can write in.

Romance fiction is defined by several essential rules and conventions that help shape readers' expectations and drive the story's emotional impact. At its core, the romance genre requires a central love story, where the romantic relationship between the protagonists is the main focus of the narrative. There must be emotional conflict or obstacles that challenge the couple and create tension, but the story is typically expected to end with a satisfying resolution—often a "happily ever after" or "happy for now." I would add that this is a requirement. A romance that does not have a HEA ending will likely be rejected by fans of the genre and violating it could cost you your livelihood, if not your life.

Additionally, romance novels rely heavily on character development and chemistry, ensuring that readers can invest in the protagonists' journey and root for their union. While sub-genres may introduce specific tropes or settings, all romance fiction adheres to these foundational guidelines to deliver a compelling love story that resonates with its audience.

Some Other Genres

Mystery: Mystery stories revolve around solving a crime or uncovering secrets, often featuring a detective or amateur sleuth as the protagonist. The rules of this genre require a clear central mystery, clues that readers can follow, and a logical resolution where the solution is revealed and explained. Fair play with the audience is important, meaning that all necessary information should be available to the reader, even if cleverly disguised. And while a mystery does not have to revolve around a murder, the terms *mystery* and *murder mystery* are generally interchangeable in fiction. ('It's a mystery' usually means somebody got killed.)

Some Authors In The Genre

- Agatha Christie, *And Then There Were None*
- PD James, *the Adam Dalgliesh series*
- Walter Mosley, *the Easy Rawlins series*
- Michael Connelly, *the Harry Bosch series*
- Louse Penny, *Chief Inspector Armand Gamache series*

Science Fiction: Science fiction explores speculative concepts rooted in science and technology, such as advanced societies, space travel, time travel, futuristic developments, and not the ever-present AI. The rules of sci-fi require internal consistency, plausible world-building, and logical extrapolation from current knowledge. The story must adhere to the rules of its invented world and address the impact of science or technology on individuals and societies. Readers will notice anachronisms (elements or details that don't belong in the time period you're describing), or inventions that seem jarring to the world you've created. (The world we live in increasingly seems like something readers from just a generation ago may have dismissed as too improbable.)

Some Authors In the Genre

- Hugh Howey, *Wool (Silo series)*
- Frank Herbert, *Dune*
- William Gibson, *Necromancer*
- Octavia Butler, *Kindred*
- Kim Stanley Robinson, *Mars trilogy*

Fantasy: Fantasy fiction features magical elements, mythical creatures, and imaginary worlds. The genre's rules demand coherent world-building with consistent magical systems or supernatural elements. Even if the setting is fantastical, the internal logic must be maintained, and characters' motivations and actions should feel believable within the established universe.

Some Authors In the Genre

- Brandon Sanderson, *Mistborn series*
- George R.R. Martin, *A Song of Ice and Fire*
- N.K. Jemisin, *The Broken Earth trilogy*
- Patrick Rothfuss, *The Kingkiller Chronicle*
- Sarah J. Maas, *A Court of Thorns and Roses series*

Horror: The primary goal of horror is to evoke fear, dread, or unease in the reader. Rules of the horror genre include the use of suspense, atmosphere, and sometimes graphic or psychological terror. The story must maintain tension and provide a sense of threat, often exploring themes related to the unknown or the monstrous, and can end with resolution or lingering uncertainty.

Some Authors

- Joe Hill, *King Sorrow*
- Shirley Jackson, *The Haunting of Hill House*
- Chuck Wendig, *Black River Orchard*
- Stephen Graham Jones, *The Buffalo Hunter Hunter*
- Carmen Miria Machado, *Her Body and Other Parties: Stories*

Historical Fiction: Historical fiction, among my favorite genres, is set in a real past era, aiming for accuracy in setting, customs, and events while blending fictional characters and plots. The genre's rules require careful research and authenticity, ensuring that historical details and social norms are faithfully represented, even as the narrative weaves in invented storylines.

Some Authors

- Nev March, *The Silversmith's Puzzle*
- Nathan Harris, *The Sweetness of Water*
- Mary Renault, *The Persian Boy*
- Hilary Mantel, *Wolf Hall*
- Toni Morrison, *Beloved*

Thriller: Thriller stories are built around suspense, excitement, and high stakes, often featuring danger, chases, or conspiracies. The rules include a fast-paced plot, escalating tension, and twists that keep readers on the edge of their seats. Characters are typically placed in peril, and the resolution should deliver a satisfying payoff to the buildup of suspense.

Some Authors

- Robert Crais, *the Elvis Cole and Joe Pike series*

- John Sanford, *the Lucan Davenport 'Prey' series*
- Gillian Flynn, *Gone Girl*
- John Connolly, *the Charlie Parker series*
- Paula Hawkins, *The Girl on the Train*

Literary Fiction: Literary fiction emphasizes character development, themes, and stylistic writing over plot. The rules are less rigid but focus on exploring the human condition, nuanced characters, and thought-provoking ideas. Literary fiction often challenges conventions, offering depth and complexity rather than adhering to strict genre formulas.

Some Authors In the Genre

- Margaret Atwood - *The Handmaid's Tale*
- Katherine Dunn – *Geek Love*
- David Foster Wallace – *Infinite Jest*
- Alice Walker, *The Color Purple*
- James Baldwin, *Giovanni's Room*

Young Adult (YA): YA fiction is defined by its focus on adolescent protagonists and themes relevant to young readers. The rules of YA include age-appropriate content, coming-of-age experiences, and accessible language. While YA can encompass any genre, the emotional journey and personal growth of the main character are central to the narrative.

Some Authors In the Genre

- John Green - *The Fault in Our Stars*
- Suzanne Collins - *The Hunger Games*
- Veronica Roth - *Divergent*
- Angie Thomas - *The Hate U Give*
- Judy Blume – *Are You There God? It's Me, Margaret*

Something to Try

Describe the genre(s) you write in, or want to write in, and why. If you write mysteries, what got you interested in them in the first place? What other genres do you write in, or want to explore, and why?

Inside the Outline: Using Your Trusty Map

The eternal question: to outline or not to outline. It's not especially challenging to write a short story without an outline, if you know where you're headed and what the story arc is. But anything requiring the sustained effort and continuity of a novella or novel means you should work with some kind of outline. It can be as detailed or as threadbare as you want it to be, as long as it helps you structure your story and stay on course.

I always know my ending—who killed the victim, who survives, and the end point of the story. That works for me, but it's not how everyone goes about it. I enjoy the discovery of writing, to sometimes be as surprised as the characters are when something unexpected happens, so I work with just a few chapters outlined and then keep going from there. I make notes. I scribble dialogue. I open my phone and add some fleeting idea to a list of them I can return to or discard.

The Master Document or Bible

I create a single Word document when I first start working on a story and fill it out as I go, adding to it, but I use it as a way to focus myself. An outline is not a straight jacket. It's easy to get hung up and frustrated trying to outline too much, and if I tried to do this for an entire book, chapter by grueling chapter, I would probably lose interest. I love to *write*, to get to it, but I need a basic map.

Using an outline for a novel provides a structural backbone that can enhance both the writing process and the final manuscript. One of the main benefits is clarity—an outline offers a bird's-eye view of your story, helping you organize key plot points, character arcs, and major themes before you dive into the prose. With an outline, you're less likely to get lost in the middle of your novel or write yourself into narrative dead ends. It can also help ensure that pacing remains consistent and that each chapter serves a purpose in advancing the story. *Every major event and plot turn must advance the story.* Just as there are no coincidences, there is no place for extras, whether it's people or narrative tangents. Stay on the road you're building.

Outlining allows you to identify weak spots in your plot early and make necessary adjustments before investing time in drafting full scenes or chapters.

Another advantage of outlining is efficiency. By mapping out the story ahead of time, you can streamline your writing sessions, focusing on bringing individual scenes to life rather than constantly wondering what should happen next. This can be especially helpful in overcoming periods of writer's block (keep reading for more on that), as you always have a guide to return to. Additionally, an outline serves as a reference point as your novel evolves, making it easier to keep track of subplots, character motivations, and continuity details. For writers who juggle multiple projects or write over long periods, having an outline means you can pick up where you left off with less friction.

There are many methods for outlining a novel, and the best approach depends on your personal style and needs. Some writers prefer a detailed chapter-by-chapter, listing the events, character objectives, and turning points for each section. Others use broader strokes, outlining only the major acts or key scenes, leaving room for discovery along the way

Ultimately, outlining is a tool, not a constraint. It's there to support your creativity, not stifle it. You might begin with a broad skeleton and fill in details as you go, or you might revise your outline multiple times as the story takes shape. The process can be as formal or informal as you like, so long as it serves your writing goals.

Writer's Block

It leaves a bad aftertaste just saying it, and while I avoided the term for many years, I've made a certain peace with its place in my life.

What does writer's block mean? It means I'm stuck, and I'm having difficulty finding my way to the next part of the story. I can know my ending without having a clear idea how to get there. The hero triumphs! The antagonist is vanquished! Okay, but how? And what are the plot points that get me and the reader from the first page to the last?

One trick I've used for years is a simple digital timer you can find in the kitchen gadget aisle at a grocery story. I set it for 45 minutes and write, or work on a project, or outline, until it goes off. If I'm in the middle of something when it starts beeping, I keep gong until that paragraph, or that scene, or that piece of this particular puzzle is in place.

I still use the term writer's block sparingly, because the more I claim to have fallen victim to it, the more power I give it. *The only way out is through.* If you can't keep the writing going, make notes. Work on your characters and your action points. Do something that will maintain your discipline.

Something to Try

Do you experience writer's block, or 'stuckness?' What is that like for you, and how do you deal with it? Do you have any methods for working through it?

A Matter of Perspective: Point Of View

Who is telling your story? You, of course. It's coming from your imagination. But unless it's autobiography or memoir, the less the reader is aware of you the better. If you've ever been reading something and you suddenly think, 'Oh, that's the author talking,' you'll know what I mean. An example might be some comment about the state of politics or the world. Try to make it clear it's the character who holds this opinion ("To Harold, it seems as if the world is falling apart") and not you. The author should be behind it all, while the main characters tell the story.

Are we being told the story by a third-person narrator, or by a character herself? Whoever is narrating provides the point of view, either from the distance of a storyteller, or head-on in the first person.

More About POV

- Point of view (POV) determines who is telling the story and how much the reader knows about events and characters.
- First-person POV uses "I" and lets readers experience the story intimately through a single character's eyes.
- Third-person POV uses "he," "she," or "they" and creates distance between the reader and the characters.
- Omniscient POV allows the narrator to know everything about all characters but can be confusing if not handled skillfully. This is rarely used today and should be avoided unless the author is very skilled at it. Mishandled, it can reflect poorly on the the writer.
- Shifting POVs (multiple perspectives) can offer depth but should be clearly separated to avoid disorienting

the reader. If you use this, keep the shifts to their own chapters. Never shift POV during a scene.

- Choosing the right POV impacts how readers connect with characters and interpret the story's events.

Furthermore

Point of view is a foundational tool in fiction writing that shapes the reader's experience. The choice between first person and third person narration impacts the level of intimacy and objectivity in your story. First-person POV allows readers to get inside a character's head, sharing their thoughts and emotions directly, but it can limit what the reader knows to only what this character experiences. Third-person POV, on the other hand, gives the author more flexibility to describe scenes and other characters, but it requires skill to maintain consistency and avoid confusing shifts in perspective.

The use of multiple POVs involves switching perspectives between chapters or sections to provide a broader view of the story world. However, shifting between points of view within a single scene can break immersion and confuse the reader. Ultimately, the choice of POV should serve the narrative, highlighting the story's themes and deepening readers' engagement with the characters. Consider carefully whose eyes the reader will look through, as this decision will shape every aspect of how your fiction is received.

First-person is the POV many new writers use because it's the easiest and it's natural to start writing, "I … *did this, said that, went there*." A lot of mysteries are written in the first-person – in my opinion too many. Simply mimicking the writer's idea of what a hardboiled detective sounds like and attempting to imitate them is not something I would recommend. I've reserved first-person narrative for very distinct characters whose stories I think could only be told by them.

First-person storytelling, like good dialogue, is not easy to do well. *You are not the character*. If you choose to write fiction in the first-person, be conscious of yourself coming through—your attitudes, phrasing and speech patterns—when it should be the character.

Something to Try

How do you intend to write your story? First-person? Third-person? Describe why you are making this choice and what constraints it may require of you as the storyteller.

Creating Suspense / Keeping Those Pages Turning

"I couldn't put it down." The five words I most like to hear as a writer of mysteries and popular fiction. I believe my job includes being an entertainer. I want to *entertain* the readers, meaning I want to draw them in. I want them to keep turning the pages, in some cases unable to stop reading, because they want to know *what comes next.* There are some techniques we can use to build suspense, which is usually at the heart of it.

Suspense includes atmosphere as well. *A dark alley.* Those three words alone conjure images and emotions in most readers. It's not just an *alley.* It's dark, with shadows and movement we can't quite discern in the distance. Among the things we imagine as we peer into it:

- lurking (as in something lurking beyond our ability to see it)
- isolation (is the protagonist alone? Are there others venturing into this dark alley, or waiting there?)
- danger
- the unknown

Darkness often implies the unknown, because we cannot see into it, or our vision is limited. The suspense can be heightened further by adding more details that create a sense of dread and suspense: Is the character following someone into this dark alley? Does she hear sounds? Does she smell things, perhaps unfamiliar or even unpleasant? Is this a dark alley where something else bad has happened? Is she in pursuit of someone? Is she in a position where the dark alley is her only way forward?

Remember Your Senses

Employ all your senses. Whether it's narration or dialogue,

remember to see, hear, smell, touch, and taste, describing each of them that comes into play. What does the room you've taken us into look like? What do you hear in the room? What, if anything, do you touch in the room, and how does it feel? Is there an odor to the room – sweet, acrid, pleasant, offensive?

Sample (*A House In The Woods*):

The following is a short passage from my horror novel, 'A House in the Woods.' Annotations are underlined in brackets.

... That's when the sound came. At first she wasn't sure she'd heard anything. One of her discoveries living in the country was how noisy rural life could be. Birds, crickets, scurrying animals and the ever-present deer, all made for a symphony of nature just outside their windows. Sometimes she heard feral cats fighting. Sometimes the lonely, mournful sounds of creatures she could not identify. But tonight she heard what sounded like scratching. [The scene is set: she's awake and alone (her husband is sleeping). We have a description of the countryside at night: feral cats, crickets, lonely, mournful creatures.]

At first she thought it was outside, and she kept turning her head, trying to locate its source. She willed herself to complete stillness and realized it was inside the house. [Tension, as she tried to identify the source of the sound and where it was coming from. And then ... *inside the house*.]

She turned to Jeremy, about to wake up him and ask him if he heard it. He was sound asleep, depleted from another day's commute and an eight hour shift solving computer problems. She decided against it, letting him get the rest he needed. She did not want to look foolish, rousing him from sleep to confront a mouse.

After listening for ten minutes—she could see the time on the nightstand clock—she slipped out of bed and headed into the hallway, grabbing her robe on the way.

The sound was more distinct now, but still muffled. She followed it into the kitchen, where it became clearer. From there she walked quickly, feet bare, to the open basement door.

That door was closed, she thought, staring down into the darkness. *I'm sure it was. Wasn't it?* She'd kept the door closed ever since Willie [a cat from previous chapters] had taken the liberty of breaking into their home. It hadn't happened since, but there was something about an open basement door leading to a rickety staircase that unsettled her. [The door had been closed, but now it's open. Who could have done that?]

She stood at the top of the stairs.

The sound came again.

Scratching.

Laurel pulled the dangling overhead string, flooding the staircase in dull yellow light. [And we find ourselves in the dark alley.] She'd asked Jeremy to replace the bulbs with brighter fluorescent models, but he hadn't got to it yet.

It wasn't a cat, that was certain.

What is it then, Laurel? she asked herself. *A raccoon? A* rat?

She considered getting a broom to protect herself from whatever animal had found its way into their basement when the sound stopped.

She cocked her head, listening.

Hearing nothing for a full minute, she made her way down the steps. She flipped the light switch at the bottom of the stairs, filling the room with light.

They hadn't used the basement for storage. There was the washer and dryer Laurel had been using after cleaning it up, and the old desk, but other than that the basement looked exactly as it had the first day they saw it.

Something drew her to the archway, that strange *door* where it shouldn't be. [This is a bricked up archway they'd been told was just part of the old house.] They'd not given it any more thought, forgetting about it amid all the other things that mattered in their new life. Now she was standing in front of it, staring at the bricks that framed the arch. The door itself, if that's what it was, was constructed with smaller bricks, many with the cement holding them in place crumbling and dusty.

Laurel thought it looked less like an entrance and more like a wall meant to keep something in.

Then she heard it again.

Scratching, from the other side.

That's impossible, she thought, staring at the bricks, trying to decide if it was the sound of an animal's claws or, *impossibly*, the sound of digging.

She stared at the wall, then said something she had no intention of saying, no intention of *thinking*: "Who's there?"

The sound stopped.

The lights went out.

Laurel screamed.

[END]

Suspense can be sudden, short-lived, or sustained. We build it by imagining it: live it in your mind as you write the scene; use effective words and descriptions, including internal monologue if it's appropriate. (Laurel keeps envisioning things about the sound, the basement, the archway.)

You can also add to the suspense by ending chapters in a way that poses questions whose answers can only be found by reading the next chapter. Did she live through this? Is she going to regret her decision? But be sparing with this device. If every chapter ends with a sentence or two requiring the reader to continue, it can feel too deliberate. It's better to have the reader *want* to turn the page than obviously forcing them to. ("It would be a fight to the death, but which of them would survive?" only works once.)

Dialogue Is the Illusion of Conversation

It may seem difficult to define what good dialogue is, but you know it when you read it. Just as importantly, you know it when you *hear* it. One of my personal dictums is that **writing is listening**. Call it magic, call it nonsense, but I hear almost everything I write a split-second before I write it. That's what we mean by developing a good ear, and not just a good voice. This is especially true with dialogue. Characters in books don't speak the way we do in real life. We falter, we hesitate, we often communicate in incomplete sentences. And we rarely talk in ways that will make a listener—in this case the reader—want to spend as much time as it takes to finish a story.

Dialogue is an illusion. Good dialogue convinces us we're hearing authentic conversations, when what we're really hearing is a bit of magic: the trick of sounding authentic when it's really more a form of music. Focus on the essence of what your characters need to say, trimming away unnecessary words and tuning their exchanges to reflect personality, motivation, and the context of the scene. Listen for how your characters might speak and let their unique voices shape the way dialogue unfolds.

Another key to writing compelling dialogue is to ensure that each character's speech is distinct and consistent. Pay attention to vocabulary, cadence, and even regional or cultural quirks that might color their language. Avoid having all characters sound alike; instead, consider their backgrounds, ages, and emotional states, and allow these factors to influence how they communicate. Good dialogue is an opportunity to reveal character traits and relationships without relying on exposition—let what people say and how they say it do much of the storytelling heavy lifting. At the same time, avoid dialect. Don't try to write with a drawl, or to sound like people you imagine talk from various regions or locations. In most cases, just write in a straightforward language and let the reader translate it in their heads. Otherwise it can be very jarring.

Remember that dialogue should serve the story. Every exchange should move the plot forward, deepen character development, or reveal important information. Avoid long stretches of idle conversation or dialogue that doesn't have a clear purpose. If you're unsure whether a scene's dialogue is working, read it aloud to catch awkward phrasing or unnatural patterns. Dialogue, when done well, not only sounds believable but also draws readers deeper into the world you've created, making them feel as if they're overhearing conversations that matter.

Some Dialogue Samples

The following examples of dialogue were graciously provided to me by authors Bruce W. Bishop (Uncommon Sons: A tale of deceit, diversity and discovery (Families' Storytelling), Icarus Press; Michael Craft (Desert Getaway (A Dante & Jazz Mystery, 1), Brash Books; and Ann Aptaker (Cantor Gold Crime Series, Bywater Books) for use in my workshops. I've also included an example of own. These are used with their permission.

Hearing is Believing

Listen to your dialogue. Just like you do with narration, pay close attention to what your characters are saying. Do they speak distinctly? Are you taking a line of dialogue that would be awkward in normal conversation and smoothing it out, economizing it?

Always listen to what you're writing. And read writers you consider skilled at what you do: what makes them good for you? Is it their style? Their craft? Their ability to keep you engaged? Read *poetry*. Poetry can teach us economy, sound, and word choice. Read short fiction. Read essays. Read *everything*, and learn as much from it as you can.

1) From Bruce W. Bishop's *Unconventional Daughters*
Icarus Press
Copyright Bruce W. Bishop
Published by Icarus Press

Katarina and Collan settled in the backseat of a taxi, their steamer trunk securely fastened. A throng of cabs surrounded them, and seemingly more people than the population of Yarmouth were bustling around the busy 42nd Street terminal.

"Fares are now regulated, ladies," the bespectacled cabbie informed them just before pulling out into the traffic. "I'll have to charge you fifty cents a mile and I reckon that the seaport district is almost five miles from here."

Collan gave Katarina a concerned glance as they were on a strict daily budget.

Katarina winked at her and then turned solemn when she spoke to the driver.

"I completely understand, sir. But you'd not be aware of the benevolent mission my sister and I are embarking upon tomorrow. Indeed, we are taking the cremated remains of some of the unfortunate victims of the Titanic back to their loved ones in Norway," she said. "You see, we've traveled a great distance from Nova Scotia at our own personal expense. Our ship leaves in the morning, and I...".

She gasped slightly, as if overcome with emotion.

The cabbie was fairly new at his job and had not yet become the jaded chauffeur he later personified; one who has heard it all. He rubbed his chin and adjusted his glasses, and then turned to Katarina.

"I guess I could charge you just a small portion of the regular fare. You're kind souls to reunite family members, so to speak." He paused, thoughtful. "You know, it's people like you who are a credit to our country," he said.

"Oh, no, we're from Cana —", Collan began, as Katarina nudged her foot.

"Cannader, Connecticut," Katarina finished, not wanting to lose the discounted rate. "Thank you very much, sir. You are a true gentleman."

2) From Michael Crafts's *Dante & Jazz mystery,* "*Desert Getaway.*"
Copyright Michael Craft
Published by Brash Books

"I've chosen this exchange between Dante O'Donnell (a gay white man working as a concierge at a vacation-rental outfit) and Jazz Friendly (a straight Black woman who is an ex-cop now struggling to establish herself as a private investigator). Their past encounters have been toxic, but now they're meeting over coffee because she has an idea that they might be able to work together." – Michael Craft

Jazz suggested, "Just do your normal job. But if you discover a situation where I might be useful, let me know. Clue me, and I'll follow through. You don't even have to *recommend* me."

"I dunno, Jazz. That's just not—"

"I'm not asking a *favor*, Dante. I'd pay you a finder's fee for clients who hire me." She named a figure.

I gave her my best poker face.

"I know, I know," she said, "it's chump change—not like you could quit the day job. But it's tough getting established, and with summer coming, it'll be worse. So I need the work. And I thought maybe *you* could use some extra cash, too." Pointedly, she asked, "That old Camry still running?"

"It gets me around."

"It's a shitbox."

She was right. I slipped her card into my wallet, telling her, "I'll keep you in mind."

"Perfect." She cracked the faintest smile. "So how was he? The Brazilian."

It hadn't been an hour. The sense memory of Isandro's sweat was still with me. "He was ... great," I said with a shrug.

She studied me for a moment before asking, "Is this 'the boyfriend'? Mr. Right, maybe?"

"Just a neighbor." Winking, I added, "We're neighborly."

"Christ, Dante. Know what's wrong with you?"

"Plenty," I assured her. "But what's *your* theory?"

She crossed her arms. "You think with your dick."

Not nice, I thought. I would never have phrased it that way, but I couldn't deny it. Since my teens, I'd gotten by on what they used to call sex appeal, which made it sound almost wholesome, like those toothpaste ads. It worked for a while—still did, to a degree—but after so many years, where did it get me? Dorky jeans. A cramped apartment sharing a common wall with a deranged rat terrier. And a shitbox Camry.

3) **From Ann Aptaker's** *Hunting Gold (Cantor Gold Series)*
    Copyright Ann Aptaker
    Published by Bywater Books

Sig puffs on his cigar. The tip glows red again, burning through the billow of smoke that briefly veils his face. "This Angeli situation must not be allowed to continue," he says. "The killings of father and daughter, one right after the other, it's the sort of thing which attracts the wrong kind of attention. Do you understand, Cantor?" He doesn't expect me to answer. He expects me to understand the implications of that wrong kind of attention. Satisfied that I do, he keeps talking. "And I am not happy that whoever is behind this is involving you in a way that is involving me. You were right to assume he knows of our meeting with Miss Angeli this morning. The question is, what's to be done about it."

"First we have to find the guy," I say.

"And you are taking steps to that end?"

"I'm poking around, yeah."

"Have you turned up anything useful?"

"Possibly," I say. I take a smoke from my pack of Chesterfields, light one up, let the tobacco do its soothing number while I settle into a conversation with the most dangerous guy in town. "It seems Miss Edie Angeli had a fling with Handy Dave Handy, who was handy enough to get her pregnant. I couldn't find anything definite about what happened to the baby, but it looks like she probably terminated the pregnancy."

Sig's only response to this news is to take a draw on his cigar. After an exhale of smoke and a silence so thick I could choke on it, he finally says, "And how would this connect to you? I don't see you as someone involved with babies." His head tilts back, his mouth opens, and he gives me his soundless laugh. That laugh's been giving me the creeps since I was a Coney Island kid and he'd have his thugs scoop me up from the shoot-'em-ups and bumper cars, then brought to him so he could either scold me or laugh about my beachfront pillaging.

When the laugh stops and he resumes his usual menacing self, I say, "Good question. I don't know how it connects to me. I'm still looking into it."

"You see, that is your problem, Cantor. You can't get the answers quickly enough because you insist on working alone. Oh, I know you have that young genius on your payroll. The kid's rather good at digging up information, I understand. But you do the legwork on your own, Cantor."

"What would you have me do, Sig? Join a street gang?" I say. "Even back in my juvenile delinquent days I was never much of a joiner."

"You don't need to join a gang to make use of it, Cantor. Why not make use of the biggest gang in town?"

"Are you offering me your services, Sig?"

His smile could curdle milk. "You are not thinking big enough, Cantor. The handful of people in my immediate organization hardly constitute a gang."

"Tell that to the poor suckers whose heads your guys knock around."

He's not happy with my pushback. I can tell by the way he takes another pull on his cigar, a long draw, his face expressionless behind the glow of the cigar's burning tip. After his exhale, he says, "Never mind the heads whose owners have gotten in my way, Cantor. Use your own head. What is the biggest gang in town, the gang which has been after you for years, but which I can—and often do—steer in another direction."

I stub out my smoke in the ashtray on the small glass table

beside my chair. I could really use a drink, a hefty shot of booze to smooth the way for the least favorite words in my vocabulary to come through my throat. "The police. You're talking about the police."

"I am talking about the police."

The following is a scene with dialogue from my novel 'Open Secrets: A Maggie Dahl Mystery.' Active words and notes are underlined, with annotations in brackets.

"Oh, that's Shanna Delaney's essay collection," Maggie said. "I promised this young woman I'd have it signed and mailed to her."

"Can't she do that herself?"

There was a tone of unpleasantness in Gerri's question. She did not care much for the book's author. Shanna Delaney was a fixture in town and had an expansive sense of her own importance ... In Gerri's opinion, Delaney had little use for anyone who wasn't there to flatter her. If you didn't want an autograph, why were you speaking to her at all?

"She was visiting from Maryland with her husband," Maggie explained. "They left town yesterday, and she asked me if I'd get the book signed and sent to her."

"And you said yes, of course."

"Of course."

"You're too nice," Gerri said. [indicate at least every few sentences who is speaking]

"I'm a business woman. 'Nice' is part of the job description." [these are ways to introduce or reinforce who the character is and how she thinks]

"Well, I hope she bought something."

"It wouldn't matter if she didn't."

The conversation stopped for a moment. Weighing her words, Maggie asked, "Have you and Tom considered ..."

"Considered what?"

"You know, living together."

Gerri sighed. "I know you want to get rid of me."

"That is not true!" Maggie protested. "I've gotten used to you."

"Like you've gotten used to Checks."

The difference, Maggie thought, is that Checks is a cat she

expected to care for the rest of his life, while Gerri could pack her belongings and move. She did not say this.

"Where is he, by the way?" Gerri asked <u>between bites of toast</u>.

"In a window somewhere. Or on a pillow. Those are his first two choices."

The same scene with no color, action or character.

"Oh, that's Shanna Delaney's essay collection," Maggie said. "I promised this young woman I'd have it signed and mailed to her."

"Can't she do that herself?"

"She was visiting from Maryland with her husband. They left town yesterday, and she asked me if I'd get the book signed and sent to her."

"And you said yes, of course."

"Of course."

"You're too nice."

"I'm a business woman. 'Nice' is part of the job description."

"Well, I hope she bought something."

"It wouldn't matter if she didn't," Maggie said. "Have you and Tom considered ..."

"Considered what?"

"You know, living together."

"I know you want to get rid of me."

"That is not true! I've gotten used to you."

"Like you've gotten used to Checks."

"Where is he, by the way?" Gerri asked.

"In a window somewhere. Or on a pillow. Those are his first two choices."

[END]

The lines of dialogue are the same, but all the color has been drained from them. There's nothing active (sighed, explained, protested), and nothing that really informs the characters or story.

We paint with words. Words are our palette. Without these other elements, we're creating silhouettes when we could be creating fully realized paintings.

Past Is Prologue: Exposition (Use As Needed)

"Exposition is the description or explanation of background information within a work of literature. Exposition can cover characters and their relationship to one another, the setting or time and place of events, as well as any relevant ideas, details, or historical context."

Use exposition sparingly as a way to offer details of the characters' past and present, as well as the story itself: How did we get here? Who and what do we need to know about? How is the scene being set? Over-use of exposition can keep the action from progressing and leave the reader feeling bogged down in extraneous details. Used skillfully it creates atmosphere, context and forward movement.

Remember: *Writing is listening.* It can be very helpful to hear what you write. Whether you choose to read your own writing out loud, or you speak it internally as you write it, pay close attention to how it sounds. You can get a sense of the flow. You can tell where you need pauses (if you pause, you may need a comma), and if a sentence is too long. You can pace what you're writing. You can see and hear how many times you've repeated a word. And you can spot clumsy or awkward sentences. *If it sounds awkward, it reads awkward.*

Some Examples

The following examples have been provided by authors Michael Craft, Anne Aptaker, and Bruce Bishop, as well as a few from my own books, with bracketed notations.

1) **From Bruce W. Bishops *Unconventional Daughters* (historical fiction)**
   Publisher: Icarus Press

If there was one part of the job he hated, it was having to process adoptions. He disliked the administration involved, and he knew that some children — through no fault of his own, of course — ended up in circumstances much worse than those they had known.

At the age of 75, he wearied of the daily routine of his spiritual calling. He hoped today might turn out to be one of beneficial closure, and dare he presume, happiness for all involved, including a measure for himself.

[In these two brief paragraphs, we learn: the character hates his job, it includes processing adoptions (which he finds tedious), it is administratively burdensome, and children often pay the price by ending up in worse circumstances.

We also learn he is 75, weary, and has a spiritual calling (of some sort). He hopes today will be different, and that he may somehow find a measure of happiness. This is a lot of information skillfully provided in four sentences that read as if they were meticulously chosen. It sets the scene and provides a complex character in uncertain circumstances, all in what might have been done with an entire page in someone else's hands.]

2) **From Michael Crafts's** *Dante & Jazz mystery, "Desert Getaway."*
Publisher: Brash Books
Copyright Michael Craft and Brash Books

"As an example of exposition, I've chosen the opening of the book, which establishes the tone of the narration as well as the setting. It leads

directly into the "now" of the story, when a voice speaks over the intercom." – Michael Craft

Palm Springs was *back*, baby!

Like a doddering, once glamorous diva, the town had limped out of the twentieth century in need of some serious dolling up. Gone were its glory days as a fabled getaway during Hollywood's golden age. Gone, too, was its later, seedier heyday when swinging crooners and affable mobsters held court from their corner booths at white-linen supper clubs.

The future, alas, was looking dim for the sunny desert oasis. But then, quietly at first, an influx of new settlers arrived, bringing along their stylish pizazz, a fresh outlook, and extravagant sass. Before long, the town grew into a gay mecca that would rise from its doldrums with a full-throated promise of fun, fun, *fun* for all— leathermen and bachelorettes alike.

I fit right in. Not only that, but when I moved here a few years ago (with the man who would later divorce me), I discovered a side of Palm Springs they don't promote to tourists— the darker side—where deadly sins take root in the sand and thrive in the warm nights. This so-called paradise does indeed have its serpents, and not all of them are reptilian. Others are metaphorical: the serpents of greed, betrayal, and murder.

But none of those unpleasantries were on my mind last February as I approached a rental house with my slim folder of paperwork. I rang the doorbell, then waited under the soaring, cantilevered roof of a boulder-lined entryway.

A voice crackled over the intercom: "Yes?"

[This is an example written in a semi-hardboiled style (note words like "diva," and "dolling up"), whether or not the character is a detective. It provides a perspective on Palm Springs as having once been glorious but fallen to seed ... until now. Perhaps it will rise again like a phoenix in the California desert. We also learn the character has a dim view of the people they've experienced there. And the story is moved forward by the character approaching a rental house and buzzing an intercom, through which a voice says, "Yes?"]

3)   From Anne Aptaker's Hunting Gold (The Cantor Gold Series)

Publisher: Bywater Books
Copyright Anne Aptaker and Bywater Books

The note's folded up and snug in my coat pocket when I arrive at Hartmann's Warehouse, a big brick nineteenth-century building with tall grimy windows along a shadowy stretch of Washington Street. There's nobody around at this hour, and except for a dark prewar Dodge parked at the curb and a beat-up two-tone three-year-old Chevy parked across the street, the area's deserted and quiet. The only action comes from random pages of discarded newspapers skittering along the cobblestones or flying around in the wind off the river. The only sound is the middle-of-the-night-music of empty whiskey bottles and beer cans rolling in the gutter.

The light of streetlamps is cut through by the High Line tracks throwing a hard pattern of dark and light slashes on the pavement and across the brick face of the warehouse. The light shines in glittering blades across the warehouse windows and cuts through the faded Hartmann's sign. Mists of steam rising through manhole covers and curling into the harsh light gives the warehouse the sort of charm Dracula might find cozy.

[This is not only first-person narrative, but also present tense ("I arrive"). It's dark. Pages from discarded newspapers "skitter" along the cobblestones. Empty whiskey bottles and beer cans roll in the gutter. Two paragraphs that provide rich details, painting a picture of a street most people would not want to go down. But Cantor Gold is there, for a reason we must keep reading to find out.]

4) **The following examples are from 'Open Secrets: A Maggie Dahl Mystery' and 'A House in the Woods 2.'**
Copyright Mark McNease
Published by MadeMark Publishing

Maggie had been a widow for just over a year. David Dahl had died in his sleep from viral myocarditis, an inflammation of the heart muscle. He'd mistaken its symptoms for heartburn and a shortness of breath he had dismissed as nothing serious. He'd thought there was no reason to see a doctor, insisting he would feel better in the morning, but what he'd been in the morning was dead. Maggie went to sleep next to the man she'd shared her life with for twenty-four years, and woke up alone. Completely, permanently alone, in the way only those who outlive their soulmates know.

[This tells us a pivotal event in the main character's life: the sudden death of her husband. Everything else flows from that: why she is living where she lives, what happened to bring her to the moment of the story, and ultimately why she chooses to solve murders, something she most likely would not have done had her husband lived. Life with and without him are parallel universes, and once he dies she inhabits only one. It also opens the door for a recurring theme of grief and loss, and how she processes it.]

A House In The Woods 2

The first house they'd bought, a small rural dwelling Laurel affectionately called "the house in the woods," had served its purpose for the first year they'd lived in the area. Several miles from Strickland, the house had been cozy but not appropriate for a growing family, even if they'd only grown by one. Once Laurel had the money from her books and the sale of the rights to them, and Jeremy had focused on his corporate career, they'd had their dream home built, then sold their house to another young couple.

The decision had become final when Laurel discovered she was pregnant. Having a child had been both a source of anticipation and a source of conflict for them over the course of their relationship and marriage. Early on, neither considered themselves ready to raise a child, and Laurel sometimes questioned if she really wanted to. Pressure from their parents, especially from their mothers, had been applied and ignored many times—it was just something most mothers seemed to be anxious about, as if producing a grandchild was irrefutable proof that the marriage would succeed. Or it was an extension of the human need to believe life would go on forever, if only through descendants. They had resisted the pressure well enough that when Laurel became pregnant after moving to New Jersey, they were surprised and ready for a child to enter their lives.

[This book is a sequel, and this passage lets us know they had lived in a different house when they'd first moved to this town, that Laurel has money from her book(s), that they'd had a new home built, and that they'd had a child, after resisting pressure from their families for some years. It brings us to the present, and the strange events that have begun to happen.]

Creating worlds that translate from our imaginations to the written word is a process that involves many moving parts: character creation, point of view, outlining, dialogue. It's very much a puzzle whose pieces we don't know we have until we begin to put them in place. Bit by bit they come together, and at the end of it we hopefully have a cohesive, compelling whole from what had been fragments in our minds. After editing, revising, polishing, and proofreading, we can step back, take a deep breath, and hit 'publish.'

Side Plates: Getting Input, Mentors, and Peers

Many people encourage and support us. Fewer still are the mentors, teachers and guides who keep us going and steel us for the long haul that is the writing life. I've lost two of my most important mentors: one who died 19 years ago, and one who died more recently. Both were critical to my ability to stay the course all these years. We learn from mentors, teachers, and peers.

Mentors

Mentors offer us more than just guidance—they provide a steadying influence throughout our personal and professional journeys. Their experience allows them to see pitfalls and opportunities that we might overlook, helping us navigate challenges with greater confidence. They encourage us to push past self-doubt and remind us of our strengths, especially when the path ahead seems uncertain or overwhelming. Their support often extends beyond advice, including practical feedback, emotional reassurance, and a belief in our potential when we need it most.

Moreover, mentors help us grow by sharing their own stories of success and failure, teaching us valuable lessons that can't be found in textbooks. They challenge us to think critically, stretch our abilities, and refine our craft, whether we're writing, creating, or building something new. Their influence is enduring, shaping not only our careers but also the way we approach life's complexities. And they often become lifelong friends. I'll always cherish the long conversations I had with Bob Delegall, whose laughter was as valuable as his insights into craft.

Writers Groups

I currently facilitate several writers groups, including three that focus on thematic journaling. Two other groups are held at local libraries and are open to anyone who writes or wants to write. I tell the participants that I consider it my role to be an encourager: to create a space where each of them can explore their own creativity through writing. There are certainly more focused and advanced writers groups, but this is what I do and what I want to offer.

Many writers groups provide critical feedback on manuscripts, short stories, and long-form writing. Perhaps a participant brings in a chapter or excerpt from what they're writing, shares it with the group, and gets input. You can find a group whose dynamics and focus work for you. They provide both skill development, 'other pairs of eyes' on what you're writing, and personal connections. *Writing is a solitary art.* It's a communication between our imaginations and a keyboard, typewriter or notepad. It is not a collective effort, until we share what we've written. It can be an important way of figuring out your story, or your characters, or where you're going with it. Writers groups can be a vital lifeline to a community of like-minded individuals.

In addition to sharing your writing, you may also benefit from networking opportunities, learning about publishing trends, promotional strategies, and even collaborating on new ventures. The emotional support and encouragement found in these groups can be essential for overcoming self-doubt and writer's block, while also celebrating each other's successes. Ultimately, writers groups are a lifeline for many, providing both the practical tools and the sense of belonging that help writers thrive in their creative journeys.

Who Reads Your Story?

This is a personal choice. Many people use 'beta readers' who read an Advanced Reader Copy (ARC) draft of your manuscript and provide feedback that can be as general or as specific as you ask them for. ARCs can also be pre-publication, nearly-complete versions of a book sent to reviewers, bloggers, and industry professionals before the official release date.

Everyone Is a Critic

When deciding who to get feedback from, whether it's one person or ten, remember that a lot of people will want you to write their their book instead. Trust the people you show your work to. Be prepared for criticism, and be prepared to ignore some of it.

Writing is Re-Writing

My books go through a half-dozen polishes by the time they're ready for the public. Notice I said polishes. One of my methods for getting unstuck is to go back and polish what I've written, starting with the first chapter. There generally is very little revision of the story, but it helps me re-build momentum and I'm able to crash through whatever barrier was in my way. There's a reason it's called a first draft. Be willing and able to write at least three before you consider it publishable.

Section Three will be about taking that leap from a final manuscript to product pages and royalty reports.

They're Alive! Creating Vivid Characters

Memorable fiction has always been filled with memorable characters: The narrator in Poe's 'The Tell-Tale Heart' hearing the beating heart of the man he'd killed and buried beneath the floorboards. Scout Finch, the young narrator in Harper Lee's 'To Kill a Mockingbird.' Celie telling her story through letters in 'The Color Purple.' And one of my favorites, a character named Olympia 'Oly' Binewski, born with albinism and dwarfism into a family of circus performers in 'Geek Love,' by Katherine Dunn.

Good characters, and certainly great ones, not only move a story forward, but they give it color, depth and motivation. When we encounter vivid characters, they quickly become alive for us. They assert a life outside our own imaginations, while always being dependent on them. Let's face it—they're not real—but they beg to differ as they step off the page and into our line of sight.

There are characters who drive multi-book series and become so familiar to their fans that we can't imagine a book world without them. Michael Connelly's character Harry Bosch comes immediately to mind. I've been reading those books since Harry's debut in 'The Black Echo' back in 1992. Twenty-five books later, and I worry that Harry will eventually die. What will I do then? Who could possibly fill that void? (I also enjoy long-running series because in most cases the character ages *with me*. Harry and I were both thirty years younger when we first met.)

Something to Try

Before we go further, take a few minutes and identify two or three fictional characters you've always remembered. What was memorable or remarkable about them?

- What is the character's name?

- What book or story or series is the character from? Try to stick to fiction (as opposed to film or TV).

How do you imagine this character looks? How do they sound?

Understanding Key Elements Of Character Creation

In many ways we are the sum of our parts: our worldview, our biases, our fears and hopes; the things that make us angry, and who we love; what matters to us, and the way we use language. Our histories—perhaps especially our childhoods—also shape us in ways that influence the choices we make. *And the choices we make create our stories.*

Who your protagonist is will determine how they respond to circumstances, and each response sets the next in motion. A story isn't just 'what happens next.' It's also 'how do my characters react to what happens, and how does that reaction pave the way for the next step and the next.'

A character who gets blamed for a murder she didn't commit will do everything in her power to prove her innocence, and in the process reveal the true killer. Is this a mystery, in which she methodically pursues the truth? Instead of being accused, is she an amateur sleuth, or a hardened homicide detective, doggedly chasing down increasingly relevant leads? Or is this a thriller, in which her life itself is in danger, and saving her own life may depend on finding or confronting the true villain? To create vivid characters is to create the potential for vivid stories.

The Character Biography: Developing Multidimensional Characters

A character biography can be as detailed or as sketchy as you'd like—as long as it accomplishes what you want from it. When I first wrote plays, my process included extensive character biographies that ran as long as ten pages or more. I would detail everything about a character, divided into categories that included their family life (past and present), schooling, physical appearance including any traits or disabilities, emotional life, psychological life, on and on. As I became more prolific, I needed less in the way of detailed biographies and more in the way of sketches. Our writing minds can fill in the rest. But at least a few paragraphs on each main character, and many minor ones, is essential in creating a cohesive narrative.

Following are a short version of a character biography list, a long version, and a paragraph version.

A Sample Character Biography (Short Version)

- Name, age, and basic physical description
- Family background and relationships (childhood and present)
- Key personality traits and dominant worldview
- Major fears, hopes, and motivations
- Important past experiences or formative events
- Education and occupation
- Distinctive mannerisms, habits, or speech patterns
- Core values, beliefs, and what matters most to them
- Primary goals or desires driving their actions in the story
- Internal or external conflicts shaping their journey

A Sample Character Biography (Long Version

Physical Characteristics

1. Full name(s)—married name, pre-married name (if applicable)

2. Date of birth (age)

3. Height, weight, build

4. Hair color, eye color

5. Distinguishing facial features
    ("She was born with a cleft palate that was repaired" — how does that affect her speech? Her appearance? Her self-image?)

6. Scars, birthmarks, tattoos
    ("He has a rose tattoo on his wrist" — why a rose? Does he try to conceal it with long sleeves? What is its sentimental value?)

7. Physical disabilities
    ("One foot is shorter than the other, causing a slight limp")

8. Type of clothes, how they wear their clothes
    ("He wears baggie clothes to hide his weight" — why is he self-conscious about this? Was he picked on? Does he judge himself over this?)

9. Race / Ethnicity — and does it matter to his/her story

10. Distinguishing mannerisms
    ("She 'talks with her hands' a lot")

11. Are they in good health, poor health, *irrelevant* health (is it germane to the story)?

Personality Traits

1. Are they more optimistic or pessimistic?
    ("He considers himself an optimistic nihilist")

2. Are they introverted or extroverted?

3. What bad habits do they have?
    ("She smokes one cigarette a day behind the house")

4. How do they display affection?
    ("He flinches at public displays of affection")

5. How do they want to be seen by others?
    ("She wants to be considered fair and open minded by her subordinates")

6. How do they see themselves?

7. Strongest character trait, weakest character trait?

8. How competitive are they?

9. What is their greatest fear?

10. What are their biggest secrets?
    ("He believed if anyone knew about his past they would consider him a threat")

11. What are their idiosyncrasies?

Family Life

Now and Then

1. Is their family NOW big or small, who does it consist of?

2. Was their family THEN (growing up) big or small, who did it consist of?

3. What is their perception of family?

4. Do they have siblings?

5. What are their relationships with their parents and sibling(s)?

6. Do they have any pets?

Past and Future

1. What was your character like as as a child?

2. Did they grow up rich or poor?

3. Did they grow up nurtured or neglected?

4. What is their greatest achievement?

5. What are their ambitions?

6. What is their best childhood memory?

7. What is their worst childhood memory?

8. Did they have an imaginary childhood friend?

9. What are their strongest childhood memories?

Love Life

1. Are they in a relationship?

2. How do they behave in a relationship?

3. What is their sex life like?

4. Have they ever had their heart broken?

Conflict

1. How do they respond to a threat?

2. How do they perceive strangers?

3. What are their phobias?

4. Who are their enemies, if they have them, and why?

5.

Work Life

1. What is their current job?

2. What are their past jobs?

3. What are their hobbies?

4. What is their educational background?

5. What is their socioeconomic status?

Spiritual Life

1. Do they believe in the afterlife?

2. What are their religious views, if they have any?

3. Are they superstitious?

4. How would they like to die?

Values

1. What lines do they have that they won't cross?

2. What lines do they have that they won't allow others to cross?

3. What is their view of 'freedom'?

4. What's their view of lying?

5. When did they last make a promise?

6. Did they keep or break their last promise?

Daily Life

1. What are their eating habits?

2. Do they have any allergies?

3. Describe their daily routine

4. Do they sleep well? Are they a restless sleeper?

5. What keeps them up at night?

6. What do they think would bring them peace?

How To Use A Character Biography

A few dos and don'ts to help you get the most out of a character biography:

Do:

- Browse the questions to get a sense of the sections and character information you think is needed.

- Pick out the questions that you find work best for you, and use them to create your character's backstory.

- Disregard any questions you don't think are relevant to your character.

- Allow your mind to roam freely; if a question inspires you to write a brief scene from that character's history, go right ahead.

- Dialogue: this often helps to get a clearer focus on a character. Allow them to speak to you and give you examples of their 'voice' when you're creating them. Well-crafted characters will put words in *your* mouth.

- Understand that your in-depth knowledge of the character will bleed into your writing, even if the vast majority of this information is never written in your manuscript.

Don't:

- You don't have to answer all of the questions for any given character.

- You don't have to go through the questions in order.

You don't have to use all of the information in your story. Some, if not much, of what you detailed will not be used. It's a way of painting a focused picture of the characters before introducing them to your story and the readers.

The Paragraph Version

This is my current method of creating characters. It works for me, allowing me to create a basic vision of each character and letting more details about them emerge in the writing.

Matthew Leland: A 12-year-old boy living in Kingwood Township, New Jersey, Matthew is characterized by his curiosity and youthful innocence. He is often caught exploring the woods around Old Hollow Road, eager to learn about the natural world around him. Despite the challenges at home, he maintains a resilient spirit and a desire to find joy in simple things.

Charlie Leland: At 36 years old, Charlie is Matthew's father. His struggles with heavy drinking have impacted his family life, often leading to unpredictable behavior. Despite his personal issues, Charlie is a complex character who occasionally shows moments of tenderness and concern for his children, revealing a more vulnerable side beneath his rough exterior.

Martha Leland: A 35-year-old mother, Martha manages her mental health by taking antidepressants. Her caring nature is evident in her efforts to keep her family together amidst the difficulties they face. She often acts as the emotional anchor for her children, striving to provide stability and love despite her own struggles.

Micah Parry: A 12-year-old only child, Micah lives on Old Hollow Road, just half a mile up from the Lelands. His parents, David and Becky Parry, are doting and attentive, providing a stable and nurturing environment. Micah is friendly, curious, and enjoys spending time outdoors, often exploring the nearby woods and engaging in local activities.

Location Context: The Lelands and the Parrys reside in the rural setting of Kingwood Township, NJ, on Old Hollow Road. Their proximity to the Horse Road Gun Club adds a distinctive element to their neighborhood, where community interactions and outdoor activities are common, especially hunting and guns. The area is characterized by its quiet, forested landscape, fostering a close-knit community atmosphere that can be deceiving for the purposes of this story.

Peter Brightly (the protagonist): A 42-year-old antique dealer residing in Lambertville, Peter is known for his sharp mind rather than his cheerful disposition. His name, ironically, does not reflect his demeanor, as he is seldom bright in mood but consistently insightful and thoughtful. Having experienced an amicable yet challenging divorce, he remains in Lambertville, where he owns a well-established antique shop. Peter is a familiar face in the local community, often seen at the hiking club alongside Lilly and Hugh Carver, who gifted him a cherished walking stick. He is a dedicated father to twin teenage sons, Raymond and Jonathan, who live with their mother in Doylestown and stay with him every other weekend.

Susan Fleming: A 43-year-old woman living in Doylestown, Susan is the ex-wife of Peter Brightly. Their divorce was straightforward and not too turbulent, leading to her moving out of their shared Lambertville home. She chose to keep her maiden name and has maintained a cordial relationship with Peter, especially concerning their children. Susan is a responsible and caring mother, balancing her personal and professional life while supporting her sons' growth and education. She has, however, taken to seeing a new man, which creates a growing friction in the story.

Raymond and Jonathan: Both 14 years old, Raymond and Jonathan are twin brothers navigating their teenage years. Raymond is more outgoing and adventurous, often eager to explore new hobbies and social activities. Jonathan, on the other hand, is more reserved and academically inclined, preferring quiet time and reading. Despite their differences, they share a close bond and enjoy spending weekends with their father, Peter, engaging in outdoor activities, exploring antiques, or simply relaxing together. Their relationship with their mother remains strong, and they are well-adjusted teenagers with a bright future ahead.

Three Characters Walk Into a Bar ...

Writing scenes with multiple characters and more than two people speaking requires some finesse. Be sure it's clear to the reader who is speaking, and that the action is not hard to follow. Anything that takes the reader out of the world you've created— such as having to backtrack and re-read sentences for clarification—will affect their experience.

When crafting scenes in fiction with multiple characters, it's essential to ensure each character's presence and purpose are clear to both the writer and the reader. Distinctive voices, motivations, and actions help prevent confusion and keep the dialogue dynamic, while careful attribution of speech (dialogue tags to indicate who is talking) and movement maintains clarity. Balancing the interplay between characters allows readers to follow the scene without losing track of who is speaking or acting.

The View from Here

There are more ways to consider Point of View besides the essential perspective of the narrative. Point of view also means how the characters see the world. This is part of character creation. Is you character hardened and cynical, or naïve and trusting? Is she dogged? What does she think of the world she lives in? *What makes her tick?*

Spend time creating characters with something to say, and something they want. Sooner than you think, they'll be telling you what to write.

In the Mind of the Beholder

Trust the reader's imagination. Don't over-explain, and avoid inserting your own biases into the story, unless your character shares them with you. If you're making an observation on the state of the world, make sure it's clear your character thinks this.

Be aware of consistency with your characters throughout the story. Whatever evolutions they may experience in the course of their journey, your characters need to speak, act and think in a consistent manner.

New Worlds Yet to Be Imagined

There's an undeniable joy in building fictional worlds—a sense of limitless possibility where imagination is the only boundary. Creating a new world allows writers to shape landscapes, societies, and rules, breathing life into places previously unimagined. Each detail, from the streets of a dystopian city to the quiet rituals of a small town with dark secrets, serves as a canvas where the author's ideas flourish. The excitement grows as these worlds become rich and textured, inviting readers to step inside and explore alongside the characters.

World-building also offers the satisfaction of discovery, both for writer and reader. As characters interact with their environments and face unique challenges, the world reveals its complexities, evolving with the story. One of the great joys of writing is having a character or a situation surprise us. It's the kind of 'what just happened?' moment that makes writing the magical experience it is for many writers.

Inventing these worlds means orchestrating every element, from history and geography to the mythologies that bind them together. The process is a celebration of creativity, where every decision, twist, and invention deepens the immersive experience—not just for those who read the story, but for those who write it as well.

Populating Your Worlds

Create your essential characters, and don't be afraid to invite new ones in to play. In some ways writing can mirror real life: you're not always completely certain who is going to walk in the door. As long as they don't take the story and run off with it, it's part of the fun—or the tragedy, depending on what you're writing—of the whole process.

Subject To Change

Characters, like people, do change, especially when the forces of circumstance and plot pressure them to. And while we remain pretty much who we're always going to be after we enter adulthood, neither our characters nor we are completely fixed.

In some genres it's the arc of the character's growth/change that is the heart of the story. This is not all that true in mysteries. Your crime solver may not be all that changed when the murderer is apprehended and your protagonist is on to the next case. But characters do learn about the world and themselves, and certainly about other characters, as the story arc heads toward its conclusion.

In the Company of Strangers

To reiterate: a living-breathing character has a mind of their own. They can and will surprise you. A well-created character is ultimately an enigma, just like people. We think we can read their minds because we made them up from our own, but don't be afraid to let them teach you something, or scare you, or break your   heart.

Something to Try

Write out three characters you've either created or want to create. Give them a mission, and say why they are inseparable from your story—even if you haven't yet determined what that story is.

Doing It All: Self-Publishing With KDP
(Kindle Direct Publishing)

Now that you have a final draft of your manuscript, the heavy lifting begins. You may want to start by ignoring the voices: both your own internal voice that could be telling you this is all too much, and the external voices that sometimes tell you you're not a 'real' writer if you're publishing your own work.

Poppycock! And how often do I get to say that?

There will always be a snobbishness in the publishing world. Like many other industries, the ability of creators to produce and market our own work has posed a threat to traditional publishers. And while it's true that anyone can publish now, it's also true that the cream rises to the top. If your books are good and people want to read them, you'll find an audience. Even when you're traditionally published *you will still have to do all the work*. Unless you're a name author, or you've written that rare debut everyone's talking about, publishers will invest very little money in you. You'll still have to do book readings, events, marketing, postcards, bookmarks, flyers, interviews, podcasts, panels, and constant promotion.

A quick story: I wrote a literary novel 25 years ago that was recommended to one of New York's most well-known agents. She liked it so much she call it literature—and what youngish author doesn't want to hear that his novel is *literature*. I saw myself profiled on NPR, with lines a block long at bookstores across the nation. What I got was a handful of publishers (St. Martin's Press, HarperCollins, Penguin) who 'almost' bought the book. Well, that counts as much in publishing as it does in horseshoes. By the time I finished a second novel that agent had passed me off on a junior agent, and soon afterward neither of them was returning my calls.

Ten years later I wrote a murder mystery and decided to publish it myself. If I sold enough copies I'd write another one. And here I am 15 years on with at least that many books out—

three mystery series, various other writings and books, and almost as many audiobooks.

I like having control of what I earn. I like seeing every unit (book) sold on my KDP dashboard, as well as other dashboards, too. And I really like the monthly, direct-deposited royalties. Have I gotten rich? Have I even made a decent living? Some months yes, some months no, but that's the nature of the beast. The upside is that I'm not waiting for sales reports from a publisher and the occasional royalty check. I also don't have to sell enough books first to pay back their advance, which is how it works. It's just not the path I want for myself at this point in my life and writing career.

Are you ready to do it all? Can you ignore the voices telling you it's too ripe for failure? And can you stop thinking of it in terms of success and failure at all? *For many of us, writing is a passion.* You've heard the adage 'Do what you love' all your life. But no one ever said you'd get rich doing it. Do what you love precisely because you love doing it.

Brave No-So-New World

Self-publishing really took off in 2007 when Amazon launched its Kindle Direct Publishing platform. It revolutionized the publishing world, with forces for and against it. It also made the world we know today possible. Ebooks, paperbacks, and hardbacks can all be done by authors themselves now. There are plenty of other publishing platforms (IngramSpark is the biggest player for bookstores and libraries), but I've primarily used KDP for 15 years so that's what we'll focus on.

Self-Publishing Versus Traditional Publishing

'Traditional publishing,' a term you'll often hear spoken with an air of superiority, is how most people refer to mainstream publishers, whether it's a giant like Random House, or one of many smaller publishers, including boutique publishers. The main difference for our purposes is that a divide still exists in the minds of publishers and to some extent the reading public between books published traditionally and those that are self-published. There will probably always be a stigma attached to self-publishing: old worlds and old ways die hard. Many authors still thrill at being able to announce they've signed a contract with a publisher, or gotten an agent. There is a cache to it that far outweighs the monetary benefits, especially if you're not in it for the money or you've accepted you'll never get rich as a writer. But it's worth repeating: Unless you are a best-selling author, you will be doing it all but the publishing part yourself anyway. You'll still be your own primary promoter, advertiser, and tireless advocate. If you want readers, you'll be just as busy however you're published.

Agents, Rejections, And The Validation Shuffle

If you're looking for an agent or a publisher, the first thing you should learn is to take 'No' for an answer. The writing life can be as hard on the psyche as it is on the budget. But if you accept that being told no is just another way of saying 'Next!' then you're off to a good start.

You Are Your Own Empire

It can't be stressed enough that when you self-publish, *you do it all*. You are your own empire, however small or large that becomes. You advertise, you blog, you interview, you read, you sell, sell, and sell some more. If you're like me, you do your own book covers because a graphic artist is far outside anything resembling my budget. But be cautious: bad book covers reflect poorly on the author and the publisher—you! If you have some graphic arts skill you can try it, but don't put out something that looks like you made it on Canva during your lunch break. There are people who can help you with a book cover for a reasonable fee.

Have A Website And A Subscriber List

Take what you do seriously. Get a website, even if it's a basic design for one book. Start a subscriber email list. I use EmailOctopus. Mailchimp is a very well-known service, but they increased their pricing several years ago and had many authors moving to lower-coast alternatives. There are others, and you can compare pricing plans. I have a fairly steady list of 1700+ subscribers. Many authors have more, and many have less. Do what you can to drive people to the site and/or subscribe. You can use BookFunnel, a good way to give out ebooks and grow your list. There are other services as well, and you can even do giveaways directly with something like PayHip. I have a storefront there, and offering a free ebook is an easy option.

A Word On Giveaways

The reaction of many authors to giving away their books—specifically ebooks—reminds me of that attitude of superiority I often sense when someone talks about traditional publishing. I know it seems counterintuitive to give your books away, but it's a good way to grow your subscriber list, and to find new readers. If you believe what you've written is good, and even more so if you have a series or multiple books, think of a giveaway as dropping leaflets from a plane over a community of book readers. The truth is I probably would not have sold those books anyway, but giving them to potential buyers is a completely free way to find them.

It Takes Money To Make Money

If you're self-publishing to get people to read your work, and then connect with more, you have to be willing to part with some money. Unless you hit the literary jackpot and someone with a huge following recommends your book, the odds are very high it will disappear in the obscurity of search engine and algorithm hell. Remember, there are hundreds of thousands of books out there, and the primary way yours will get noticed and hopefully purchased is through your own efforts. It requires a degree of tireless, and tiring, promotion. It also requires a willingness to invest in yourself.

Ads, promotions, BookFunnel, even giveaways. We have to spend money to get our books in the hands and on the devices of readers. Ultimately it's a plus and minus equation, and the balance is what we earn. You have to ask yourself if it's worth it: if you want to put your books out as audiobooks, will you sell enough of them to justify paying hundreds of dollars to a narrator? Will you sell enough ebooks and paperbacks to recoup what you've spent promoting them?

It's important to take the long view. If you intend to write and publish more than one book, develop the patience required to wait six months, or a year, or possibly longer, to make it to the plus side of the ledger. And do your research on services that offer to help you reach an audience. BookFunnel is good for growing an email list, but not so much for selling books. BookBub is the one subscriber service out there that generates a significant return, but they reject 8 out of 10 submissions, if not more. Be wary of the others. Like vanity presses, don't believe the promises or the hype without reading about the experiences people have had with them. Making money from other people's dreams can be a lucrative business.

You're Ready to Publish, Now What?

Choosing a Platform

- Platform diving: The ease of KDP (Kindle Direct Publishing)
- Why I use KDP
- Other Platforms: IngramSpark, Barnes & Noble, Kobo, SmashWords, and more
- Exclusive versus 'wide'

In The Beginning

None of this happens without a publish-ready draft. How you get there—writing, editing, beta readers, proofreading, line edits—is a lengthy process, and here you are near the finish line. Now what?

Why I Use KDP

I use Kindle Direct Publishing and have for over a decade. Before KDP absorbed CreateSpace, I used it strictly for paperbacks. Now, everything lives inside one dashboard. For many independent authors, KDP remains the fastest, most intuitive route to publication, with global reach and a low barrier to entry. The interface is familiar, the learning curve is manageable, and the support materials are plentiful.

There Are Other Options

You can publish through a distributor like IngramSpark or Draft2Digital (formerly Smashwords). Draft2Digital pushes your book out to all major retailers: Kobo, Apple Books, Barnes & Noble Press, Amazon, and dozens of smaller outlets that you can select when you do the set up. You can also upload individually to each retailer, which gives you more control over pricing, metadata, and updates, but requires more time.

I've recently begun adding my books to IngramSpark, the biggest player in distributing to bookstores and libraries, and the platform almost all of them use. It requires a slightly greater learning curve, especially with paperback and hardback specifications for interiors and covers, but most bookstores will not order from Amazon. If your desire is to have your book ordered by and sold in bookstores (and easily added to library catalogs), you should consider learning to use IngramSpark. The good news is that you can also do both, and I do. There is no prohibition against uploading your books to KDP, IngramSpark, and any other publishing platform, but each one (excluding ebooks in most cases) will require a unique ISBN number that you can get for free from the platform when you set up your books, or use you own.

It's important to note that IngramSpark requires offering retailers a significant discount, with some flexibility in what you select. For the U.S., it's a range from a 40 percent minimum up to a 55 percent maximum. Retailers have the right to return or destroy unsold copies, which you must refund them for. You can see why many independent authors choose to publish through KDP and forego IngramSpark. It really depends on what your goals are.

For our purposes, we'll focus on KDP, because it remains the center of the self-publishing, print-on-demand universe.

A Word On 'Wide'

'Going wide' is a phrase you'll encounter frequently as it applies to ebooks. It simply refers to whether you list your ebook exclusively through Amazon (by joining KDP Select), or make it available anywhere you want to. Exclusive enrollment lasts 90 days at a time. Only ebooks are affected—paperbacks and hardbacks are always non-exclusive. But be mindful: KDP Select auto-renews, and their bots actively search the internet for duplicate listings. Even pirate sites can trigger warnings. If they find your ebook elsewhere, they may exclude you from KDP Select for a full year.

KDP Select makes your ebook available to its vast number of Kindle Unlimited subscribers. The current cost to a subscriber is $11.99 per month. That allows them to download as many Kindle books as they want. What you get from it is pennies to the page read. For some authors this can be a significant revenue stream, with writers claiming to earn as much as 30 percent of their monthly royalties from it. On the other hand, KDP owns your ebook for 90 days at a time.

The Pros of KDP Select

- Ability to run Kindle Countdown Deals and free promotions (up to 5 days per 90-day term)
- Access to the enormous pool of Kindle Unlimited readers
- Potential for steady 'page-read' revenue, sometimes a large percentage of a self-published author's monthly income

The Cons Of KDP Select

- You cannot sell your ebook anywhere else while enrolled
- Limited exposure outside Amazon's ecosystem
- Kindle Unlimited revenue can be unpredictable and vary widely month-to-month

Bottom Line

Know your goals. Are you after maximum visibility in one ecosystem, or slow growth across many? There is no right answer, just strategic choices.

What It Looks Like

Each edition of your book will have its own formatting requirements, whether it's an ebook, paperback or hardback. And while ISBNs are required for paperbacks and hardbacks, they're not generally required for ebooks. If I'm using my own ISBNs I would not include them in ebooks because it's money more wisely spent on paperback and hardback editions. Take the free one instead.

An ISBN, or International Standard Book Number, is a unique identifier assigned to books and other published materials. While most people don't know what it is, they'll find it in the front of every book they read. It serves as a uniform system to facilitate the identification, cataloging, and purchasing of books across the global publishing industry. The ISBN system was introduced in 1970 and has since become an essential tool for publishers, booksellers, libraries, and distributors.

The primary purpose of an ISBN is to provide a unique number that distinguishes one edition of a book from another. This is particularly important because a single title can have multiple editions, formats, or publishers, each requiring a separate identifier. The ISBN helps to avoid confusion and ensures accurate ordering, inventory management, and sales tracking.

Typically, an ISBN consists of 13 digits (previously 10 digits before 2007). It ensures that each book can be uniquely identified and tracked throughout its lifecycle, from production to sale and library cataloging.

If you provide your own ISBN, you can use the same one for various publishers, provided nothing about the book has been changed. Bowker is the exclusive and largest ISBN provider in the U.S.

- Official agency: Bowker Identifier Services
- Website: myidentifiers.com

- If you're based in the U.S., this is the only legitimate source for ISBNs

Be aware that ISBNs purchased through Bowker can be very expensive. A bundle of 10 ISBNs currently costs $295. That's a lot, and buying a single ISBN is currently $125. Depending on how many books you intend to publish and what your goals are (do you want to be a multi-book publisher of your own and possibly other authors' books?), it's more cost effective to get free ISBNs from the publishers. *That means Amazon (KDP), IngramSpark, Barnes and Noble, and others. Each of these is the publisher if you choose to get a free ISBN from them.* This does not mean you can't use your own imprint. I do—it's MadeMark Publishing, and the interior of my books states that, but when your book shows up on Amazon or any of the online retailers, it will say 'Independently Published,' or 'Ingram,' and so on. If you want it to say 'Your Imprint' you will need to use your own ISBN. I have begun using my own again because I publish multiple books a year and want to be more attractive to bookstores and libraries.

You will have to provide a separate ISBN for KDP, and another one for IngramSpark, Barnes & Noble, and on down the line if you choose to use an ISBN provided by them.

Let's Talk About Formatting

- ebook
- ISBNs (not needed for ebooks in many cases)
- Table of Contents: listing and linking
- Justify Your Love (side-to-side)
- A word about section breaks (a must) and tabs (avoid them)
- File Type: Word, EPUB, PDF

Ebook Basics

When you set up your book for publication, you'll be required to upload the manuscript and cover. For ebooks, most platforms accept Microsoft Word files (.docx), *EPUB files, and occasionally older formats like MOBI. For ebooks, Word or EPUB are simplest. For paperbacks and hardbacks, PDF is mandatory—it preserves layout, page numbers, and spacing.

*An EPUB file, which stands for Electronic Publication, is a widely used digital ebook format designed for easy distribution and reading of electronic books and publications on any e-reader. EPUB files adapt to various screen sizes, allowing people to read ebooks on any device, whether it's Kindle, Nook, or one of several e-readers available as apps. While there are many uses for EPUBs, you're primary concern is for ebooks. These files also allow you to distribute your ebooks yourself, whether you're giving them away or selling them.

You can convert Word to EPUB using free online tools, and EPUB files often upload faster and produce fewer unexpected formatting issues on KDP and other platforms.

Proper Ebook Formatting

You'll need:

- A title page
- Copyright statement
- A linked Table of Contents (crucial for ebooks)
- Section breaks between chapters (avoid page breaks)
- Justified text for a professional look

While requiring a title page and copyright statement may seem obvious, usually followed by a boilerplate disclaimer about being a work of fiction (or whatever genre it is), not everyone realizes that a table of contents with links to each chapter is standard for ebooks. This is because there are no real pages. You can't insert a fun bookmark with an image of Emily Dickensen or your favorite animal into you ebooks as a placeholder. While you can flag pages where you've stopped, you can't simply flip back through the chapters.

A Table of Contents with links to each chapter is a must, and should follow the copyright page. If you don't include this, you may be prompted by KDP for not having one (it sometimes says you don't have a table of contents when you do—in which case ignore that message).

You do not generally include a Table of Contents with paperbacks and hardbacks for the same reason. You don't need them. If you pick up any fiction book at a bookstore and open it, you will not see a Table of Contents. The story simply begins. An exception to this might be a text book, a how-to book such as the one your reading (!), a history book, or a book of essays. But in almost all cases you can forgo a Contents page in print editions.

Section Breaks, Not Page Breaks, And (Almost) No Tabs

While you're writing your book in Word, use 'Layout' 'Section Breaks' 'Next Page' to separate chapters. Using straight 'Page Breaks' can throw off your formatting when it's converted. Section/Next Page breaks are also very important when you're formatting a paperback or hardback interior. They are what tell the Formatting Genie to keep headers and footers continuing from the previous section (not the previous page). You'll save yourself a lot of frustration if you do this. Page Breaks can also throw off your ebook formatting.

Tabs and extra spaces can explode formatting when converted. A single tab usually doesn't cause a problem, but tabbing over several space can lead to text that looks like you put it into a blender. Use tabs sparingly, and allow your text to drop to the next line automatically. Only use 'Enter' and manual line breaks when you have to, such as separating paragraphs or sections.

Avoid the Panic!

Be sure to create and save versions for yourself:

- Final Word file
- Final EPUB
- Final PDF
- Editable cover if you design it yourself

You'll want all of these later for any possible revisions, ARC (Advance Review Copy) distribution, BookFunnel giveaways, selling directly, easy distribution, and any changes you need to make on the cover design or dimensions.

Under The Covers: Making A First Impression

Judging A Book By Its Cover

It's never too early to visualize your cover. Some authors wait until the end; others find that looking for images in the initial stages helps define the book's tone and inspire direction. I often start imagining a cover when I first begin writing, and many times design draft covers as a way to get my mind into the story.

As independent publishers and authors, budget concerns are always a priority. Having learned through experience and a lot of expense, I concluded that I would be best served by designing my own covers. I simply cannot afford to pay book cover designers or graphic artists what they charge (and deserve), so I do it myself. But be cautioned: a good cover is a major selling point. Only attempt your own covers if you have some skill as a graphic designer. Otherwise seek out someone who can do it for a price you can afford. See some of my book covers on the next page. It's safe to say I started working with images and ideas for the covers well before any of the books was finished.

Book Covers

More On Covers - DIY or Outsource

KDP Cover Creator is quick but limited. You'll find it offered when you are doing your book setup and you're required to provide a cover—your own or theirs. Most covers created with Cover Creator (or another platform's version of it) look generic. Depending on what your goals are, this is fine, but consider your options.

- Hire a designer (rates vary widely)
- Use pre-made covers with some version of Cover Creator
- DIY using licensed images and simple editing tools. *This is what I do.*

Image Sources

There was no such thing as generative AI when I started publishing. It's ubiquitous now, and while I have used AI once for a book cover (*Hell to Pay*), it remains controversial. In all other cases I have used image services and paid a very minimal license fee for the image, then created my cover using it. You can purchase images individually or in bundles (10 for $50, for example). What you cannot do ethically is 'steal' images from the internet to use as your book cover, no matter how tempting. It's worth paying $5 or $10 to maintain your integrity and to respect the work of others.

Some well-known and affordable image sources:

- DepositPhotos
- Shutterstock
- Adobe Stock

- Free options like Unsplash (always verify the license, never use someone else's images without paying for them)

If you use AI imagery, you currently must disclose it when you set up your book, depending on the platform. That disclosure does not affect approval.

Design Tips

- Choose high-contrast images that work with text overlay (always remember you will have a title, possibly a subtitle, and author name that must be readable over the image; this applies even more to the back of the paperback or hardback where you include a synopsis, recommendation, and an About the Author paragraph if you choose to do so).
- Consider color psychology (mystery/thriller may use darker tones, romance may use warm tones, nonfiction may be light or off-white). However, follow your design instinct. Capture the heart of your story in whatever colors and images work for you.
-

Always design with the paperback wraparound in mind—front, spine, back. With several books I used a solid color for the back because the front image did not lend itself to having small text layered over it. Here is a full paperback cover template downloaded from KDP (you'll need the final PDF page count before downloading this, so that it meets the exact size).

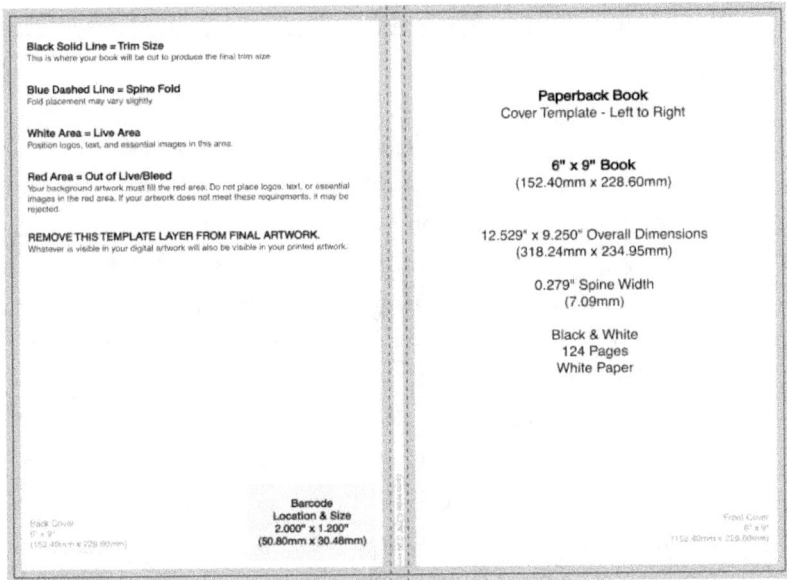

Black Solid Line = Trim Size
This is where your book will be cut to produce the final trim size

Blue Dashed Line = Spine Fold
Fold placement may vary slightly

White Area = Live Area
Position logos, text, and essential images in this area.

Red Area = Out of Live/Bleed
Your background artwork must fill the red area. Do not place logos, text, or essential images in the red area. If your artwork does not meet these requirements, it may be rejected.

REMOVE THIS TEMPLATE LAYER FROM FINAL ARTWORK.
Whatever is visible in your digital artwork will also be visible in your printed artwork.

Paperback Book
Cover Template - Left to Right

6" x 9" Book
(152.40mm x 228.60mm)

12.529" x 9.250" Overall Dimensions
(318.24mm x 234.95mm)

0.279" Spine Width
(7.09mm)

Black & White
124 Pages
White Paper

Barcode
Location & Size
2.000" x 1.200"
(50.80mm x 30.48mm)

Back Cover
6" x 9"
(152.40mm x 228.60mm)

Front Cover
6" x 9"
(152.40mm x 228.60mm)

Back Cover Essentials

- Synopsis (150–250 words max)
- Optional author bio (About the Author, which you don't have to identify that way)
- Optional praise or recommendation
- Optional author photo
- Leave space for a barcode, theirs or yours, generally in the lower right corner

Paperback Writer: Formatting For The Paperback Edition

Formatting the paperback is the hard part of preparing a manuscript for publication, although in most cases you can use the same finished PDF file for a paperback and hardback unless you change sizes. 6 x 9 is the standard, but you don't have to use that, especially if you're aiming for a children's book, poetry chapbook or something else that widely uses other sizes.

ISBNs (Those Again!)

You must have a unique ISBN for each format: if you publish both a paperback and a hardback, you will need to change the ISBN number for each of those editions.

Always include the ISBN on the front page where the copyright is listed.

Choosing A Template

You can't simply change the margins in a Word document to adjust it to a paperback interior, unless you're highly skilled and experienced at it. Interior book pages adjust the margins automatically so that when you flip the pages, the margin shifts. The best way to do this is to use an Interior Template, which you can download from KDP or IngramSpark. I've been using the same interior template for years, and simply replacing the text with the chapters of a new book (I only keep several chapters in my 'generic template' so I'm not replacing 30 or more chapters each time).

As I format a new book, *I copy and paste one chapter at a time.* Yes, it's tedious. Yes, it's necessary. If you try to copy and paste your entire book, or even several chapter, the margins will explode and you'll have different chapters with widely different margins. Take the time to get it right, and you won't have to fix it later.

PDF Conversion

Once you have a final formatted interior, you must convert it to a PDF. That is what KDP, IngramSpark and all the others will require you upload as your interior. Why? *Because these are print-on-demand books.* That means each time a customer buys your book, the publisher prints a single copy and ships it to them. You will be able to order as many author copies as you want to, and pay the printing cost, not the retail cost. You'll know the printing cost when you set up the book because it will tell you, depending on what you set your price at. For example:

- You set your paperback retail price at $12.95
- KDP tells you the printing cost is $4.25
- You pay $4.25 for each author copy, plus shipping.

Paperback formatting takes time and patience, but done correctly it will give you a book that lives forever and looks the same whether it's been bought online or sold at a book fair.

Worth repeating: Always keep editable versions of your files and don't lose track of the various drafts. Save frequently, keep a backup. It's very easy to lose track of which one you worked on last, and the final 'Publish Draft' is the holy grail. My folder for any given book may have a dozen or more files, including covers and images.

Following is a short sample from a formatted paperback interior:

OPEN SECRETS

A Maggie Dahl Mystery

*PAPERBACK INTERIOR

MARK McNEASE

2

CHAPTER One

MAGGIE KNEW WHY THE COUPLE was staring at her. It happened infrequently, but often enough for her to know the source of their curiosity: she was the one who'd found the kidnapped woman in a basement cage. She was the one who had exposed a monster living among the community. It had made her famous in a way she'd never wanted to be, and it made her feel like a stop on some walking tour of Lambertville, New Jersey. "Look to your left, ladies and gentlemen, it's the woman who brought a sadist to justice. Her name is Maggie Dahl. Remember it." She was even asked for autographs from time to time, something she found unsettling and morbid.

"May I help you?" Maggie asked the young woman. "We've got some nice spring offerings, peach preserves and our new rhubarb jam."

The woman looked to be in her thirties, dressed in leggings and a large blue button-down shirt, her long blonde hair in a single braid down her back. "We're just visiting," she said, as if that was an answer to Maggie's question. Everyone who came into the store was just visiting, even if they bought something.

The man seemed impatient, glancing at his watch and looking toward the door. If Dahl House Jams and Specialties was part of a tour, he was ready for it to end. He didn't look like he'd be leaving a tip for the tour guide.

"Take your time," Maggie said, choosing not to pursue these customers. After six-plus months in business she'd learned when to apply gentle pressure and when to leave it alone.

"May I ask you something?" the woman said, moving closer to the front counter.

Here it comes, Maggie thought.

"Of course."

The woman hesitated a moment, then said, "Does Shanna Delaney live around here?"

Maggie felt foolish. She'd assumed the interest she'd sensed

3

from the woman was about *her*—about her notoriety, her place at the center of an infamous chapter in the city's history—when it was really about another famous person who lived there. Shanna Delaney was an author whose book of essays about life in a Delaware River town had made her a local celebrity. Her follow up, a series of personal portraits of the people who lived these lives, was to include a chapter on Maggie as a big city transplant who'd left the excitement and glamor of New York City for a quieter existence. Shanna had approached her about it several months ago at the store but had not yet followed up, and Maggie suspected the essayist's interest in her had as much to do with the horrific events of the previous fall as it did with Maggie's adjustment to life in Lambertville.

The woman pulled Delaney's book out of her large, daisy-covered cloth purse, and held it up for Maggie to see. *Essays from a River Town* was a collection of a dozen pieces Delaney had written detailing the joys, and occasional sorrows, of living in a small city nestled within a stone's throw of one of America's great rivers. It presented a way of life many saw as slower-paced, more relaxed, and more fulfilling than life in the nearby metropolises of New York and Philadelphia. Maggie found the book slightly unrealistic, especially given her own experience with the dark side of small city life since moving here. But the book was popular and had attracted its share of inquisitive tourists looking for a world that existed mostly in Shanna Delaney's mind.

"I was hoping to get her autograph," said the woman.

Trying not to let her disappointment show, Maggie said, "Shanna likes to write at the River Brew coffee shop, but only in the mornings, from what I've seen. Are you in town long?"

The woman's face fell. The man looked at his watch again.

"We're leaving this afternoon," said the woman. Then, struck by an idea, she offered the book to Maggie and asked, "Could you have her sign it and mail it to me? I can pay for postage."

Maggie sighed under her breath. The only thing worse than being asked for her autograph was being asked for someone else's.

"Certainly," she said, taking the book. "Just let me write down your name and address."

"Emily," said the woman as she waited at the counter. "Emily Markham. This is my husband, Todd."

4

Go Tell It On The Mountain

Your book is out there in all its glorious editions. Now comes the selling part, and it's a slog. Be prepared to promote yourself tirelessly and at every opportunity. Be prepared to do book giveaways, especially of your ebooks, which is very easy. There is also Goodreads, but I find it clunky. The interface looks like it hasn't been updated since its launch in 2007, which it probably hasn't been. But it is a huge audience of book readers and reviewers, so make use of it. Become a Goodreads Author. You can also do a Goodreads Giveaway ($119 the last time I did one) to get your book noticed and on the TBR (to be read) shelves of a few hundred readers. It's not as effective as it used to be, but Goodreads has a devoted community.

About Those Reviewers

Never respond to a review. And if you're like me, you don't read them anymore. While it's a thrill to see a 5-star review gushing over your masterwork, it's also very risky to read a 1-star takedown who trashed you because they could, or the 'Why did I waste my time on this book?' reviews from people who think they're writing for the New York Times. Worse still are the Amazon trolls who rate your book 1-star with absolutely no explanation. Yes, they're out there. No, they didn't read the book. *Ignore them*, one and all. I'll admit to having learned some things from reviews, such as the need to tighten my prose and not use so much exposition, but once you've taken in constructive criticism where it's offered, let the rest go. Reviews can be similar to social media 'likes,' making us think they love us one day and hate us the next. Stay away.

Expectations Are Disappointments Waiting to Happen

There's nothing quite like hitting that publish button after you've set your book up. You can tell your friends and fellow countrymen that your book is now available. But be prepared to wait. Everything takes time, and publishing can be as much of a long game as writing the book was. Don't obsess over sales, reviews, or royalties. Be pleased and proud with what you have accomplished, then let time and effort do the rest.

Rejoice—you made it

Hearing Is Believing: A Word on Audiobooks

ACX Overview

ACX is Amazon/Audible's audiobook creation and distribution system. If you want to put out your book on audio, here are some basics. Begin by setting up an account with ACX, including your direct-deposit (banking) information and whatever else it asks for.

Claim your title on Amazon (it must be already published).

Follow the set up for a 'new production.' Once you get to the page where you're ready for auditions, you choose a short excerpt from your book, no more than two pages, and upload it. ACX will review it, then make it available for narrators (who ACX refers to as producers), and you'll soon be getting audition audio files that you can listen to on the platform or download.

Once you identity a narrator you like, you move into the offer stage.

Payment Options For Narrators And You

- Per Finished Hour (PFH) — you pay the narrator upfront; they will generally include a range for the fee, anywhere from $50 per finished hour to $400. Per finished hour means the final length of the audiobook, not how many hours it took them to record and prepare it, which can be three times the number of hours of the audiobook.
- Royalty Share — no upfront cost, you split the royalties evenly, after ACX takes its 60 percent cut, which means you and the narrator will split the remaining 40 percent of net sales; if your audiobook is $20, you can expect to split $8. Yes, you read that correctly.

- Royalty Plus — hybrid (recommended when possible; this means you split the royalty and also pay the narrator something for their work—I've always done this because I know how hard it is, and because what we all do has worth. Even $300 makes a difference).

I have a high regard for the profession of audiobook narrating. All the people who think you should narrate your own book, or that it's as simple as sitting in front of a microphone and reading a book aloud, have no idea what's really involved.

Narration is acting, technical editing, mixing, and mastering. Respect the craft. Provide pronunciation notes if they're needed (especially with names), and reasonable character guidance. Remain open-minded: you will never hear the voices exactly as you imagined. Also, don't micromanage. Once your narrator starts their job, don't bog them down with notes or requests to re-record something (they will deliver the first 15 minutes for your review at an agreed-upon date). After that, let go, it's in the hands of the audiobook gods.

Thick Skin and a Lot of Determination

Follow Your Dreams

Self-publishing is rewarding but demanding. Some months will feel triumphant; others will feel like shouting into the void. Success is subjective. For some it's money, for others it's holding the finished book in their hands. Know your desires and definitions early.

You are not your sales numbers. You are not your Amazon rank. You are not your reviews — glowing or scathing. Publishing is a marathon, not a sprint.

Get Out There

Attend festivals, local bookstores, senior centers, coffee shops, libraries, and community events. Even small engagements matter. Two readers can become two reviewers. Ten can become fifty over time.

Professional Organizations

Writers groups and forums are great, and depending on your goals it's also helpful to join professional organizations. Some to consider:

- Mystery Writers of America (I was on the board of the New York Chapter for two years)
- Independent Book Publishers Association (but don't join if you won't make use of their programs, spend your money wisely)
- Sisters in Crime
- Alliance of Independent Authors

There are many others, just look for them. They provide community, resources, and credibility.

Reviews and Requests

Ask friends, family, newsletter subscribers, and colleagues for reviews. You'll wait a while — everyone waits. That's normal. But don't be shy about it. Amazon doesn't even require a written review anymore. Just be aware that this may also invite trolls, who are part of the world we live in now.

And Finally ... You Are Not An Imposter

Dismiss the temptation to think you're fraudulent in any way. You wrote a book. You created something from nothing. That is accomplishment enough.

About Mark McNease

Mark McNease is an author, publisher, podcaster, and workshop leader whose work centers on storytelling in all its forms.

He writes both fiction and nonfiction, exploring genres that include mystery, the supernatural, urban fantasy, literary fiction, and recurring columns on humor, health and aging.

He is the founder of MadeMark Publishing, a subsidiary of MadeMark Media, where he publishes his own work and helps select authors offer their books to the reading world.

In addition to his publishing and media work, McNease leads writing workshops and journaling programs through YourWritePath.com, helping writers of all levels develop their voice, confidence, and creative practice. His journaling workshops have been particularly effective in helping participants rediscover the stories of their lives.

Across books, podcasts, workshops, and digital platforms, Mark McNease is guided by a belief that stories matter—that they inform, entertain, preserve history, and connect people through shared experience.

"Every life is a story, and each of us is the storyteller."

He can be contacted at MadeMarkPublishing@outlook.com
MarkMcNease.com
YourWritePath.com